MOONLIGHT ELK

MOONLIGHT ELK

ELK

ONE WOMAN'S HUNT FOR FOOD AND FREEDOM

CHRISTIE GREEN

HIGH ROAD BOOKS | ALBUQUERQUE

ISBN 978-0-8263-6672-6 (cloth)
ISBN 978-0-8263-6673-3 (ePub)

Library of Congress Control Number: 2024938897

Founded in 1889, the University of New Mexico sits on the traditional homelands of the Pueblo of Sandia. The original peoples of New Mexico—Pueblo, Navajo, and Apache—since time immemorial have deep connections to the land and have made significant contributions to the broader community statewide. We honor the land itself and those who remain stewards of this land throughout the generations and also acknowledge our committed relationship to Indigenous peoples. We gratefully recognize our history.

Cover illustration: *Etching of Moonlight Elk* by Tracy H. Seidman
Map by Christie Green
Designed by Felicia Cedillos
Composed in Chaparral Pro

For Olivia.
And the animals.
Wild and innocent.

CONTENTS

PREFACE

Do you recall the split-second, trigger-pull moments when your body took over to assert an ultimate choice and rendered you unreasonable? Was it for love? Livelihood? Power?

Did something precious shatter?

As you move through the daily maze of choices at hand, the sticky mess of in-between, can you explain why? Is desire justification enough? Or is it survival? Is there a difference?

Good. Bad. Right. Wrong. True. False. How long will you reside in the claustrophobic trap of extremes—surety tugging at each opposing end of the war rope that binds us?

What is the urge to loosen and allow, to slip beyond edges and boundaries, to refuse the containment of category? Is it a tempting invitation? Or a threatening dare? What is lost in the letting go? Who wins?

Stories inside us carry the past forward and cast the future back, like seeds saved in tiny jars hidden in earthen walls, waiting for the just-right conditions to set themselves free, swell with rain, burst forth, take root.

Does the flower know she evolved from death?

Transformation lies between here and there, in the liminal shadows.

What myths lie dormant, waiting to germinate? What stories pulse through you, seeking the absolution of daylight or the refuge of darkness?

❦

IN LATE SUMMER of 2001, when I was thirty, my grandfather and I approached a seven-acre parcel of land for sale in rural El Guique, New Mexico, near the confluence of the Rio Chama and Rio Grande and Ohkay Owingeh Pueblo. The pickup jiggled over the cattle guard and descended the driveway toward the house and acreage beyond. "Stop right here," my granddad instructed. Pappa, the realtor, and I hopped out and gazed wordlessly at the acequia below. This irrigation ditch, the San Rafael del Guique, was the first of thousands dug across the state according to Spanish Moor tradition. Ten feet wide and at least as deep, it coursed with hazy, green-brown water. Wild plum, orchard grass, and kochia weed stabilized its bank. Neither of us had seen so much water on agricultural land. Could this place begin to quench my thirst?

A wheat farmer and cattle rancher on the Texas High Plains, my grandfather was more familiar with praying for the mercy of rain from passing clouds than knowing any comfort of consistent moisture. Pappa's dryland farmer's hands were calloused from repairing combines, greasing machinery, and siphoning Ogallala water from irrigation ditches. I remember him sitting on the edge of his office chair, head bent down, slowly rocking back and forth, taking in each detail of wind, rain, hail, and high and low temperatures forecasted for the day. Could the farm keep going a little while longer?

After crossing the acequia Pappa stated flatly, "We don't need to go any farther. This is it."

"How do you know, Pappa?" I asked, a little surprised by his emphatic declaration. He was a quiet, understated observer, interjecting only when invited.

"There's water," he said. "You don't need anything else."

There began my four-year love affair with an adobe house and seven acres adjoining the Rio Grande bosque. I balanced my city profession as a landscape architect—bending nature's wildness to human whim—with my desire to grow food and work the land. The river's meander held my fledgling-farmer dreams. I carried my mother's and grandmothers' teachings about food, trying to emulate love and family through canning bumper crops of cherries, beets, cucumbers, tomatoes, and peppers. I imagined growing old between those adobe walls a foot thick, beneath the pitched roof facing south to the river. I could see my own calloused hands and the bushel baskets of heirloom crops sold at market to fund a simple living. Here I was going to live—and love—on my terms.

Land was the greatest richness, a wealth I believed unattainable for me, a woman with no business savvy and too much passion.

Much blood had been spilled in the acequia-irrigated orchards and rows of chiles, beans, corn, and squash of El Guique. This is where Spanish conquistadors tried to tame indigenous people and land. There's a deserted visitor center just a few miles north with a statue of Juan de Oñate. In 1998 vandals cut one foot off the statue, a symbolic retaliation for his brutal treatment of the indigenous people in sixteenth-century Acoma, where he massacred hundreds of Pueblo men, women, and children. Oñate sentenced every man over the age of twenty-five to two decades of servitude . . . and cut a foot off twenty-four of them. In 2020 the controversial statue was removed. Today the center is fenced off, a silent sequestration of the bronze soldier that once loomed there with his sword raised high.

The waters of the San Rafael del Guique continue to run through Pueblo land, as well as the land of the Jaramillo, Borrego, Casados and Padilla families. Everyone irrigates from the same acequias, lifting and lowering the *compuertas*—the gates that open to allow water through to lateral ditches for irrigating—to different rhythms related to each owner's acreage and corresponding water allowance.

The water flows high and low depending on winter snowpack and spring runoff. The mayordomo, governor of each acequia, watches carefully to ensure that no one withdraws too much and that those with water rights continue to irrigate per the "use it or lose it" mandate. If acequia water is not utilized to flood-irrigate crops, the rights to that water could be withdrawn from the property. I and other Anglos adopted the acequia system as well, working ourselves into a

sort of fluid lineage that has formed tributaries far beyond the conquistadors' original intent.

My Hispanic neighbors with deep, extensive roots there plowed
my fields with handshake agreements in exchange for a fresh-baked
pie. They generously demonstrated corn planting in the dark with
headlamps after our "real job" hours. "We place three seeds per hole,"
they explained, sowing the crop on time, which was dictated not by
the official last frost date of May 15 but by mid-June, when the most
threatening waves of insect pests would have passed.

In the February greenhouse I started Brandywine, Hillbilly,
Green Zebra, and Mexico Midget tomatoes; de Arbol, New Mexico
Sunrise, Big Jim and Sandia chile peppers; and *calabacitas* squash.
During the growing season of early summer until early fall, I
coaxed acequia water around gopher hole sinks and woody weed
stalks. I harvested under late summer's blazing northern New
Mexico skies, cooling my muscles after sunset by dipping silently,
neck deep, in the acequia. This place unearthed secrets long buried
inside me. In the secluded privacy of this hopeful home, I could
hear whispering voices from within that had been silenced by trying to do everything "right." Hungry, I welcomed lovers to my bedroom on the bull's blood, packed-mud floor. Dating and living with
men left me wanting for a man who would stand by me—not stand
over me.

I had tried to work a nine-to-five job, contribute to sensible
savings and retirement accounts. But I itched to expand beyond
the tight margins of convention. Something inside refused to
settle. I started and grew a business, purchased the house and
land, and made my way, writing my own rules, dismantling—and
deregulating—the suffocating good-girl "should" at my throat.

I chose to loosen the laws of defined roles and acceptable trajec-
tories through my work, the land, and my body. In these realms I
could assert an identity and fashion a lifestyle of my own.

What I didn't know how to do, I did anyway, fueled by my desire
for connection to place and the possibility of recreating what my

grandmother, grandfather and their farm had instilled. Belonging. Roots. Identity.

It was along the Rio Grande that I conceived my daughter, Olivia, from the most unlikely lust-work relationship with a Hispanic cowboy twenty-three years my senior. His wrists of copper bracelets and his sexy Spanish—"Sí, se puede"—as we connected eight-inch gated pipe melted my practical, get-it-done work mind into a tangled mess of attraction. His sharp, black mustache, rigid, olive-skinned jawline, and penetrating, thick-lashed, hazel eyes got to me. He distracted me from my sixteen-hour workdays with corporal temptation and sensory indulgences. I wanted a man, a man to share in the work of rooted land, growing heritage, and commitment to place through water and stewardship—a man like my grandfather. I wanted a man to feast on and feast with, to lick sticky fingers of tortilla-chile-dipped love. But my desire and indulgences, which blended seduction and sensible stewardship, proved intolerable, incomprehensible to the men I invited in, their families, and others who tried to make sense of me. Wanting a home and business I could cultivate as mine and relationships with men in which I was seen, emotionally supported, and celebrated proved too much to ask for and sustain.

Now, eighteen years later, El Guique is a bittersweet memory. The daily forty-five-minute commute to Santa Fe with a newborn and mid-winter breastfeeding stops on the shoulder of the highway broke me. It was all too much to handle alone: I needed to be closer to family and friends, more easily accessible to Olivia's many adopted and biological aunties at the ready to rock her to sleep or stroll her round and round while I snuck a shower or nap.

Tender morsels of me remain there years later; that place was like no other. I now have a semblance of rural living on two acres along the dry riverbed of Santa Fe. I cultivate food beyond the threshold of each door, our cat evades coyotes most every night, and a wraparound portal holds many lively meals, occasional Sunday naps, and Olivia flopped on the banco humming iPod tunes, her Levi cutoffs and tank top exposing tattoos.

We have moved on.

But I still burned for belonging, for a presence that defined me by something deeper than weekly schedules, work roles, and cultural norms.

The opportunity to hunt surfaced along with a man who showed up to help build my chicken coop in 2008. We ignited each other. Ours was a seemingly impossible love between an unlikely match. Neither of us had been married or wanted to settle into the comfort of coupledom. I imagined stoking desire in an unconventional, long-distance relationship that revolved around seasonal cycles with the animals, on the hunt. He lived that way, coming and going as he pleased, following his own migratory path.

Rationale named food, sustenance, and self-reliance as justification to learn to hunt. Somehow the logical undercurrents of cultural norms still tugged at me, and I validated my urge to hunt as an extension of practical agency. If it were just about the food, would that explanation be enough?

But a restless stirring brewed inside. What if I could expand beyond plants and the garden, beyond the supposed domain of women and venture into the world of animals, into the wild, where men prevailed? Could this man and the hunt provide a different something or someone to orbit? Could this burning within me and between us blaze deeper? Could it last?

But the burning wasn't about a man. Outside the crisp cusp of the human realm, the moon seduced me to the in-between. Here she cycled through me, rising and falling at dawn and dusk, whispering messages from the dark side. Rather than circling the hot insistence of a masculine sun, I began to attune to the more elusive, mysterious murmuration of the moon. Her subtle, cyclical wisdom of hide and reveal, light and dark, reflected to me the power of not knowing, the necessity of unknowing, and somehow condoned a deeper stirring inside. Captivated by her shadow, I allowed my own dissolution.

The animals and the dreams, as rhythmic lunar partners,

choreographed me through time and space, among nonlinear wavelengths. I, too, wanted to dance, dream, toil, live, and love at the edges of the in-between, the fertile ecotones where I could withdraw inward, retreat like an animal into hiding, and also come into full, radiant view.

Through the animals, definitions dissolved, reason was defied. Boundaries blurred. The animals got to me with their musk scent, teeth ground through grazing, hooves marred over mesas and mountains. I saw them from the inside out and, finally, began to see myself.

Their meat became my meat. Their bodies became my body. Their way became my way.

Tracking and tracing, moving in darkness, watching, smelling, listening, and following the animals, I shed the burdens of my domestic self. I peeled away skins that adhered to a prescribed grid, manufactured tick of time and picture of perfection. While the farm had welcomed me into my own earthly rhythm, body to body, skin to soil, the animals walked me farther into their world, ambled me along the arc between night and day, waking and sleeping, rational and natural.

I began to hunt in the eight ecoregions of New Mexico in 2010. Elk. Deer. Oryx. Turkey. Grouse and quail. By penetrating their bodies with bullet and knife as enigmatic communion through blood, guts, hide, and hoof, I began to see myself. Like them: uncontrollable, unknowable, and valuable . . . as is.

What I sought from these animals was food. What I have found is freedom.

Now, on daily walks with my English Setter, Opal Luscious, I traverse piñon-juniper hills, telling time through topography. I seek insight by covering miles, boot to earth, tracking, and following the whimsy of Opal's nose-to-ground, bird-scent curiosity. I never know what we may find, who will cross our paths, or what hand will be forced.

The weight of many fields and gardens tilled, furrows irrigated, seeds sown, and relationships broken slips from my shoulders. While I carry my weapons, I mosey with no particular direction, imagining the animals, wondering how they choose which way to go. What compass guides them? What do they nurture or sacrifice to survive? Do they find their way best obscured in shadowy moonlight or by the light of day? Or both?

Questions percolate, pace me, settle the urge to escape toward the extremes of here or there. How can I be a mother and a predator, a woman who gives and takes life? What reason is good enough? What, still, do I have to learn from the animals? Will the moon ever whisper her secrets into my ear? Will I know how to listen?

With the rifle pressed into my shoulder, and dreams breathing at my neck, I take in the view beyond the circular glass of the sight to the land that holds life. I look through the crosshairs of the scope, turn the lens to sharpen focus.

I see close up, then choose whether or not to pull the trigger.

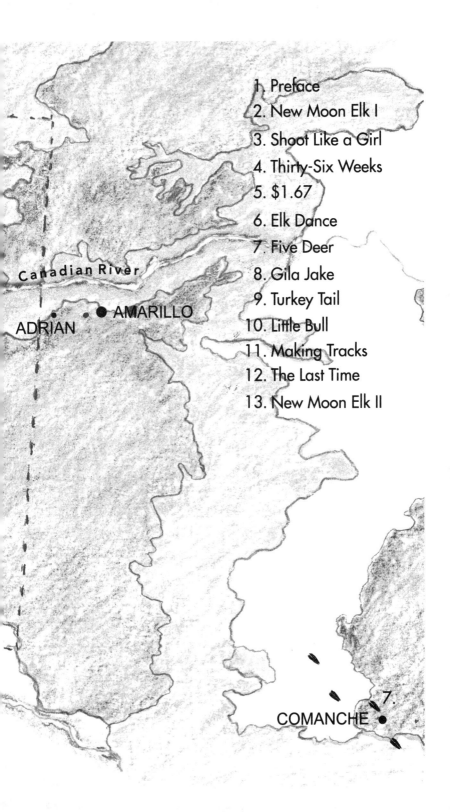

Canadian River

ADRIAN • AMARILLO

COMANCHE 7.

MOONLIGHT ELK

NEW

First lunar phase when the moon is situated between earth and sun.

The moon rests, dark, nearly invisible to the naked eye.

She is a shadow of herself.

DREAM DEFINED

A series of thoughts, images, and sensations occurring in a person's mind during sleep.

A cherished ambition, aspiration, or ideal.

Believed to be separate from what is real.

2018

NEW MOON ELK

Day One

Friday, November 2, 2018. Odometer reading: 99,065 miles. 6:00 a.m. 25 degrees. Wind from the north. Turn from Forest Service Road 125 onto Forest Service Road 124. Mile 99,070, elk tracks everywhere. Mile 99,074, park in the clearing to the south. One hour past daybreak. The moon wanes to a slim crescent. I scribble data into the lines of the notebook, handy on the passenger seat. I pay attention to how long it takes to get here, how cold it is, wind direction, how much gas is in the tank, how far I'm going and how far I've come up the dirt road from where I'm camped in the Airstream southeast of Cebolla, New Mexico. It's my first solo hunt for elk.

The weight of my marriage is lifting. I don't have to carry the fixing of it anymore. We have been separated for three months and divorced for seventeen days now. He's not here to suggest, request, or set the pace. I decide the direction of this hunt.

The legal hunting period for my tag starts tomorrow, so today will be for scouting only. I will learn new territory in Game Management Unit 51, where I usually hunt in the northeastern section. I choose the opposite side this time. I don't want each step to be a memory of what was with my husband as we traversed Kiowa Mountain, Tusas Creek, and Cunningham Canyon in prior years. He had been the one to teach me and partnered with me on turkey, elk, deer, pheasant, and oryx hunts. I want to create new memories, chart my own course.

Elk tracks crisscross the snow-covered roadway, revealing the passage of dozens of animals through the draws, creeks, and dense spruce timber, then up the ridges on their daily pilgrimage from nocturnal grazing to diurnal, north slope slumber. The snow, two days old, lies six inches in places at 9,500 feet and above. I know I'm lucky to have a hunt coincide with winter weather like this. Tracks are easy to read in snow and give me a hopeful sense of having a leg up on the other hunters who won't arrive until later this evening at the end of the work week.

Low, foggy clouds shroud the sunrise. I reach a place that looks good, near an elk route, with easy parking. Keys zipped inside my jacket. Cell phone off and in pocket. Range finder in pack, accessible in an exterior pouch, and water, snacks, maps, rope, extra clothing, hand and foot heat packs, toilet paper and mini first aid kit in the main backpack compartment. Most of the things Al used to carry for butchering and carrying out the animal, quarter by quarter, are now on my back. I mark the waypoint in the GPS unit and turn it off, placing it in the left thigh pocket of my pants. I pull my long johns and camo over-pants down to squat, peeing Earl Grey tea with cream and vitamin B12 neon yellow into the powder near the truck tire. Pants up, eighteen-pound backpack on, 16 gauge on my right shoulder (in case I spot a grouse), and binos around my neck, ready at my chest.

As my boots crunch across frozen elk tracks that emerge in steel blue light, my friend Adam's parting words from the night before repeat in my head, "The timing should be good with the moon like this and fresh snow." He had reached toward me, prompting a fist bump. "Kill!" he had said after peeling off a bite of the Ibex leg from his grill. I had stopped by to say hello, check in with this man, a good friend and hunting buddy of mine who had hunted since he was a young boy, like Al. I kept seeking out the wisdom of more experienced hunters, men, who knew more than me. Maybe I hoped their confidence and knowledge would rub off. Maybe I hoped I would receive some sort of know-how transmission—or permission—to step into the unlikely role of solo woman hunter, unaccompanied, unguided.

"Kill," I say to myself, as I make my way down the road to an easterly two-track leading to the meadows and timbers above. I slow my pace, lift the binos, adjust their focus, and scan the timbers, understory, and openings. Maybe a slight movement or elk-hide brown will catch my eye. Maybe I'll luck onto them here. These pre-dawn walks with Al into new territory were always part of recounting our story once back home, "That elk bugle we heard just as we set out before dawn was electric! I couldn't believe we got into them right away like that!" Fresh bear tracks, the poorwill's red eyes reflecting our headlamp light, the scuttle near our feet at the road's edge. Nocturnal critters are still up and about, but I witness them silently, without the whispered "Look at that!" this morning. I prefer to walk without a headlamp. I want to see as the animals do, without the aid of human apparatus. Can I be as quiet as them? As unobtrusive? Can I smell and hear as they do?

My Monday conversation with the New Mexico Department of Game and Fish's elk biologist had ignited my anticipation. "We just did helicopter surveys over that area last week. The population looks healthy. We counted 1,845 elk in the Trout Lakes and Canjilon areas. That's definitely a good spot." I recorded our forty-five-minute conversation in my notebook, so many questions answered, yet many more unasked. I didn't want to take too much of his time and didn't want to come off as totally clueless. "They may delay the rut depending on environmental conditions, but usually by no more than a week." I wonder if I'll hear the bulls bugling, and the cows calling. I want the hormone craze of the rut to skew an elk's sensibility just enough to allow a shot. If I bag one, surely I'll be a real hunter.

Maybe then I can be new. Maybe then I won't be defined by the man at my side.

Striding on, I feel my hips resist the weight of the pack, hear my stomach rumble. I stop, realizing I'm almost at the top of the drainage and have barely paused. The city's pace still informs my tempo. It will take a couple of days to slow down. The needles of the Douglas fir tickle my neck as I stand still. A motion out of the corner of my eye yanks my bino scan back to the left. An elk ear appears among dense branches. A cow steps out into the clearing, not more than thirty-five yards to the south. She heads my way, not having the benefit of being downwind to cue her to my intrusion. Her front legs stiffen straight, nostrils flare, head jerks up. She's onto me. We lock eyes, looking with curiosity at the other as if to query, "Who are you? What are you made of?" Her chestnut hide, soft, exaggerated ears, and whiskered mouth set in my mind's eye.

She is what I came for. I see her. Recognize her.

She turns sharply upslope and disappears, like a mirage. I head to the pickup, her golden rump and our encounter softening my checklist mind. My march dissolves to a trickle. I slow my descent, remind myself to take care, move with intention. Al and I would take off cross-country when hunting, both at dawn and dusk, sometimes not coming back until hours after sunset, having to navigate our way with headlamps, a map, and a compass. I don't want the stress of unnecessary risk eating at me on this hunt, nor can I afford to make careless mistakes. My daughter Olivia is only thirteen and needs me. "Don't get lost. Don't get hurt. Be smart," I remind myself like a mantra.

Back in the pickup, thirty-three degrees, wind swirling north to south, I strip layers, turn the fan and seat heaters on and tear open a bag of cashews, dried blueberries, and raw walnuts. I've already seen an elk and it's not even noon. But seeing her feels less like a hunting score than a brush with another world.

❦

AFTER MY MORNING snack I explore new territory. A change in road surface to the south piques my interest. Hopping out of the

Tundra, I descend the route about a half mile to the rim of a small lake, about two hundred yards across. Two other marshes to the north and west contrast their chartreuse sedges and rushes with the surrounding fescue and grama slope. The air is different here in this low spot, a drainage at the south end of where I walked earlier. Cooler. Hushed. I lose track of time, lie back on a sunny, dry knoll, with oaks behind me and clouds skimming my daydreams. Nowhere else to be until my belly rumbles, empty, impatient.

Lunch eventually beckons me back to the Airstream seven miles west. I notice caravans making their way into overburdened sites not far from my camp. Quads, pop-out and pop-up campers, high-clearance pickups, and trailers stacked high with tarps, coolers, grills, and shade structures clutter the clearings. They circle up around multiple fire rings and position generators nearby. I wonder how many tags are being fist-bumped before they're filled? How many guys are set to the task of putting the moves on the one elk that will be theirs?

Stomping the mud from my boots, I juggle breakfast fixings plucked from the cooler and tug the door open. The little propane stove fires up without a glitch as butter slides across the skillet. No one to feed but myself, I adjust to single serving proportions: two eggs instead of six, one tortilla instead of three. I devour a burrito of scrambled eggs creamy with pepper jack cheese and chopped green chile and wash it down with stiff coffee and cream. I study the topo maps and Google Earth images, combing the imagery for clues.

A nap is in order today. I snuggle into the down sleeping bags and heavy wool blankets. An hour passes; dreams sift through me.

The elk converge at the base of a slope, one bull leading them into the nearby bedroom whose window widens to the outer expanse. He enters; a dozen cows follow. I sit at the bed's edge, yellow spread under my thighs. They're filing in as if for an interview in a beauty pageant, stopping in front of me one by one. The bull looks directly at me, icy blue man eyes meet my stare. He has a blonde human beard, six-by-six antlers. The elk linger, eyes affixed to mine. Are they silently asking me to join them or flaunting their animal freedom? The cows follow their bull out the other bedroom door, an obedient tempo, a determined destination.

3:00 p.m. I wake bolt upright, fearing I've wasted the day and lost the elk. Geared up, propane shut off and camper locked, I head out again for the evening walk.

3:50 p.m. The first drainage, where the cow was in the morning, is mucky with melted snow and slippery soil. My eight-pound boots press into the thick ooze, leaving circular dimples from the tread. I will recognize my own tracks many times over on this hunt. I tell the time of my trips and those of the elk by how defined or diminished our tracks appear through day and night, freeze and thaw. Whose tracks cross the others? They tease me with, "Maybe this way . . ."

Following my morning route, I ease my gait. Shift to the pace of this place—slower like the shadows of clouds over hipped topography. No rush. At the clearing where the long, aspen-lined meadow meets the two-track, I spot the point of antlers. A young bull, head in the brush, grazes without distraction. There are at least six cows foraging around him, in and out of the timber shadows, unfazed by my presence. I range them at eighty-three yards and practice getting set up for a shot, lying on my belly in the snow, with the shotgun resting on a fallen aspen. One cow moves broadside repeatedly, revealing her widest self to me. The shot could have been mine at least five times over but I hold still, focused on their muzzles, tugging leaves between curled lips. It's not the time to shoot yet. The hunt opener isn't until tomorrow.

The sky blushes, exhales the day's effort and I move on, just a little farther up, before turning to walk back in darkness. A neck, head, and ears float through the fir branches. Another cow. She crosses my path, senses my presence, turns toward me. We hold the stare. She curls her lips, opens her mouth to expose her teeth, flaring her nostrils to get a scent. Who am I? What am I? She steps even closer. We hold the curious tension. I forget my boots, pack, binos, and gloves; I am as exposed as she is. Our eyes meet. At fifty yards she barks two warnings to alert the others, then turns away, cautious.

I descend, contrasting the feral feeling in my bones with the biologist's facts: "The numbers there are good. We're seeing a 40–100 calf-cow ratio and 35–100 bull-cow ratio. Numbers in the 40s indicate a productive herd." Today's observations corroborate his data. They're here. I'm settling into their rhythm but am pulled away to the rigid rationale of making the kill.

Back at the Airstream, I resist raw memories of Al and I when we were here during last year's hunt. The camper was merely a shell then, no bancos, shelves or cabinets had been built. The bathroom at the back, a baby blue curvature with old chrome fixtures, held a mirror centered above the rear window. I remember Al's mouth buried between my legs, my knees at his ears, crouching forward over him, rocking slowly on the blanketed foam mattress. I grinned at our reflection in the mirror, saying to him, "Look at us." Here, on the hunt, we didn't have to worry about muffling our sounds or tiptoeing around, being proper. I could let loose, be all woman, less obliged to conform. Here my desire to dominate and seek my own satiation first felt more allowed, aligned with the wild. Here, I began to feed my hunger.

Now the only steam the windows collect is from the green chile stew simmering on the stove. Who and what do I give my body to now?

Boots off, belly full, I set the alarm for 4:00 a.m.

Day Two

Saturday, November 3, 2018. 99,104 miles. 34 degrees. Dense fog. Hint of wind from the south. Arrive at day one's sweet spot at 5:54 a.m. Moon waning, darker sky, slimmer crescent—barely a toenail.

No more than two steps toward the drainage, a bull bugles a

high squeal about three hundred yards ahead. The snow beneath my boots now has a thick crust, having frozen over yesterday's melt. My steps are loud, clunky as I approach the clearing. Cows are here too; they're still hanging with the bulls. I need something solid to prop me up against my unchecked adrenaline. Without a more experienced hand at my back, a large aspen does the job. I lean into the vertical mass, ask for support, guidance. The tree, surely older than me, can whisper clues of wisdom. "They'll come up the low drainage, cross the clearing, and head over the ridge to the north-facing slope." At least that's what I choose to hear.

I wait, breathe, listen, and let my heart settle back inside my chest. I must remain still, rooted, until first light when I can shoot.

Hooves crunch in crusty snow twenty feet to my right. The she-elk comes directly to me, morning light revealing our outlines, the south breeze exposing truths of who belongs here.

A convoy of trucks and four wheelers blasts in, breaking through frozen mud puddles. I step away from the tree, and head toward the parked trucks. "I'm already in here," I declare to the man who jumped out and peed next to his truck. He responds dismissively, "I didn't see any vehicle." The men head in, full force, revving engines. The cow has vanished.

I walk. Scan. Stop. Listen. Walk some more. More guys accelerate toward the meadow where last evening's elk grazed. Crouched down against a spruce trunk, hidden from view, I witness their passing. Two men in pickups and two others on quads, gun their engines heading into the elk zone.

BAM BAM BAM! Three shots fired uphill. *BAM BAM BAM . . . BAM BAM,* five more fired below me. I'm surrounded by what sounds like haphazard shots, most likely at moving targets. Three men with orange vests and hats, one with a rifle, traipse through the snow, within thirty yards of where I'm crouched. I have to get the hell out of here, lest they mistake my movement for a cow's and start shooting. I slink through the trees, concealing my body behind rough bark trunks, fallen scrub and dense brush. The terror of becoming the hunted, the consequence of one stray bullet slaps me to attention. The elk head for the dense high country; I flee to the safety of the pickup.

9:30 a.m. 36 degrees.

The fog lifts. I head to the wetland, thankful to be the only hunter there. The walk to the cluster of little lakes feels shorter than it did yesterday—I'm there in a blink this time. Hours pass: I cover the perimeters of each body of water, every ridge and the flat expanse of the main lake by foot and by binoculars. I can tell the elk have just been here that morning; I decide this is the place to be at sundown. They like it here. So do I.

The morning lulls into early afternoon, my boots and pack gaining weight as I begin to feel groggy. I've been awake for six hours already. A nap is in order.

2:00 p.m. Time to return to the pickup for salami and Swiss cheese on crackers, beet and sweet potato chips, and leftover Halloween candy. The salty sweet Reese's linger in my mouth as I clear the back seat to lie down.

I'm driving up a remote Forest Service road on public land in northern New Mexico. I drive a little farther and see there, along the barbed wire fence, what looks like a mechanical bull. The kind in honkytonk bars that you put a couple of quarters in and get to ride as your rowdiest cowboy self.

It looks like a mechanical bull, but I see it's the remains of a bull elk that has been brutally slaughtered. Hunters have been here, but they weren't hunting for meat. They cut off his head and antlers with a dull saw. Rough, torn edges of flesh expose muscle and sinew below, and drying blood cakes the thick hair and hide, stains crusty snow. The spinal cord is exposed, and the hooves have been cut off too—now stumps remain at the end of legs that once ran uphill. The cuts on the legs are jagged, uneven, made with indifference. The taking lingers like a hollow moan.

An hour passes, and I wake up, chilled. The taking in the dream mimics the tone of taking here. Can I do it differently?

Two pickups and two quads zoom by. It's time to head back to the wetland for the evening's sit.

Set up on the south-facing, Gambel-oak slope, I wonder about the low, round shadows about one hundred yards before me in the otherwise uninterrupted snow. Are they tracks? Where do they lead? I lift my binos to make out what appears to be round cobblestones. Following the path of stones, my binos land on two brown rumps.

It's as if the stones had been strategically placed: at the path's end, two elk graze in the thickets, unaware of me. In a commotion I place my pack on the ground, rifle against its slouch on the soil, four 168-grain bullets in the cartridge with one in the chamber ready to fire. I lay flat and calm down enough to position the rifle. They're close, so I adjust the scope down to a five power. Crosshairs on one body, I wait for the elk to lift its head. A bull? A cow? She raises her head, gnawing the forbs and grass, keeping a watchful eye. This is when Al would have whispered instructions or assisted with shooting sticks, the range finder, or an extra rifle prop. He would be there as confident backbone to my frenzy.

But I know that this is my shot, so I range the cow at 153 yards. As I adjust the rifle to fire, she turns to the north and takes a long step toward the lake's edge. This is it. I click the safety forward to the off position. As my index finger inches to the trigger, the other elk steps out into my line of sight.

It's a calf, small enough to only have been born in late May or early June. Mother and calf are solo. My thoughts trace as many paths and directions as the compilation of tracks I have witnessed over these two days. "KILL!" and "Just take the first shot you have under two hundred yards"—admonitions from my hunting peers at home—reverberate through me.

They are tempered with the indelible flash in my mind of a heartbeat monitor line confirming a pulse.

No, Olivia needs me. She laps up homemade buttery biscuits with honey on our morning ride to school. She sips the tea I've brewed before bed. Reaching for me, she rises with skinned knees from the fallen, twisted bike beneath her on the gravel path. We have held hands, the two of us, in synchronized stride since her birth.

The mama cow must live.

This is my choice.

I click the safety back on, sit up and watch the pair with my naked eyes. Their hooves trace a relaxed path along the lake's edge and through a small opening in the oaks. Just after sunset when their shapes are no longer discernible, I make my own way out, mimicking their pace, their route. No hurry. No fear or alarm. They drift innocently to their evening destination. I return to the pickup with a heavy gut, knowing that may have been my only chance.

The mother, her calf, the close-range cows from yesterday's scout, the nonchalant bull and grazing harem. I eject the cartridge from the chamber, pull the magazine from the rifle and place it in its case in the back seat, and wonder why I've been closer to more elk on this trip than ever before.

I'm prepared in all ways to make the kill, but the hunt has mutated. They're getting to me—their proximity, their ease. No one is here to yank me back to the trigger.

I question the "You are you by the feeding you do, the body you give" that has been the DNA of my march, my toil, my loving. I have provided, served, satiated. Now, without apron or negligée, I am becoming flesh and bone, hooves and heart.

As I witness the animals, I begin to see myself.

Day Three

Sunday, November 4, 2018. End of Daylight Saving Time. What time is it? Cell phone says 4:39 a.m. Tundra says 5:39 a.m. Google says 5:39 a.m. 23 degrees. 99,122 miles. No wind to speak of. A wisp of a moon. Very dark.

I want to arrive in the dark and walk in with the elk as they migrate back to the cover of timbers from their nighttime grazing around the lake. Ice grips the water's edge. I decide to spend the day in the marshy watering hole, shifting position from one end of the finger meadow to the other, to the oak edges and the moss rock outcropping over the smallest pond. It's hard to sit still for long in the morning's acute chill. Like a little kid, I itch: "How long until I see one? What's going to happen? What's next?"

Breaking my cover, I stand, stretch, and look around. I walk a blatant path from my oak perch to the fir, stand beneath its canopy, and lift my binos toward the south side of the lake to the densest cluster of timbers. Right there, at first glance, I spot what appear to be two hind knees in a one-foot opening between smoky gray trunks. She or he is about two hundred yards away, a plausible shot if I get in position and sit still long enough. I bring my belly to lake's edge. Obscured by shrubs and shadows, I position the rifle on my pack, legs slightly spread to steady my hold, cartridge loaded, safety off. I watch through the scope for an opportunity to verify the sex and shoot.

No movement. No knees. No elk. She's gone. After approaching where she had been, looking for hints at her whereabouts, I see only perfect brown oblong turds and yellow holes in the snow where she peed.

Morning warms to afternoon. I decide to return to the Airstream to cook lunch and then gas up in Cebolla. I heat leftover green chile stew in the skillet, garden potatoes popping as the broth cooks off, sausage jumping at the clap of skillet heat. Two fried eggs, two pieces of toast, extra chile, and black coffee, then I'm off on a short half mile drive to the local gas pump. I wait for the hunter gassing up and make small talk that typically would have been Al's conversation to have. I make the eye contact this time. Solicit interaction. Raised in New Mexico, he's hunted this territory many times over. He tells me, "Yeah, I got two on that ridge right there with a bow; a couple others near Canjilon Lakes. Gotten so many, but no luck so far this time. I'm heading back to Santa Fe now and will try again in the morning." I share snippets from my past couple of days. He smiles, screws the cap back on, and concedes, "You know, sometimes it's just not yours to have."

Behind the counter, a slender elderly man looks at me with the milky eyes of age, a hint of blue rimming brown irises. I hand him the debit card as he looks me over. "You hunting?" I nod. "You know you really shouldn't be up there alone. A lady and all."

"Why is that?" I ask.

His grin pores over my camo as he runs the magnetic strip through the machine. Silence. "Well, I guess you have a gun." Another man comes in and pays for his liter of whiskey. They exchange familiar words in Spanish before he climbs back into his 1980s Nissan, which strains under the weight of fresh cut ponderosa rounds stacked high in the bed.

99,138 miles. A full tank at $2.88 per gallon. I return to the wetland, but there's no action.

Three more days left to hunt and the topo maps back at camp provide no direction, no clues.

Day Four

Monday, November 5, 2018. 4:23 a.m. 36 degrees. 99,151 miles. No wind. Whisper of a moon.

I sling the rifle over my right shoulder, like a strapped-on phallus at full attention, loaded. Hard steel at the ready. The hour and a half walk to the "sweet spot" is now familiar and slips by with familiar landmarks dotting my viewshed: the faded blue of a crushed Bud Light case, an empty, bright orange chainsaw oil bottle, and a swath of sawdust where a fallen ponderosa had been cut into thick cylinders to haul away. A spindly twig of an aspen across the path perks me up almost as much as the new elk tracks. I wonder if any of these cows have the ear transmitter the biologist told me about. "We caught about 109 by hand and placed the transmitters in the calves' ears. We do it before they're a week old, when their instinct is to hide, to stay still in the grass rather than run.

We can walk right up to them and place the transmitter." The devices relay information back to Game and Fish about the animals' whereabouts and health. "Older cows, say those that are eight to twelve years old have a lower conception rate. Prime-age cows have about 80-90 percent conception rate. They only carry one; twins are more common in deer."

Elk musk from fresh feces and urine seize my attention as I approach the clearing by the pickup for lunch. They've just been here. I follow their route, lifting my knees over crisscrossed fallen logs, turning to miss the scrape of rose thorns against my pack. I sit, listen, breathe them in.

CRASH! A bull tramples aspen limbs just forty yards away, asserting "like hell the scientists will have any say about when my rut starts or stops." This, the first week of November, is about three weeks past the prime mating season. They're still doing it, which could be to my advantage. I wait. Listen. His hooves pound me to attention.

The testosterone-fueled tantrum stops. I follow my nose, as well as driblets of poop and pee, dropped on the move by about four elk not that far ahead. I wonder how the elk—cows weighing in at 500–600 pounds, bulls at about 700–800 pounds—make their way through this type of cover without a sound. I end up at a meadow about halfway between the crossing and the wetland gem. I'll wait here.

Darkness falls in sync with my aspirations. I return to the pickup. A cow squeals in the distance as I unlock the door. They elude me.

What will there be to celebrate? To tell? Who will I be, returning home empty handed? How will I feed everyone?

Day Five

Tuesday, November 6, 2018. 5:31 a.m. 23 degrees. 99,171 miles. Brisk wind from the south. No noticeable moon.

Today I move to higher ground. With the Jemez Mountains to the west, Colorado to the north, Canjilon waking up to the south below, I chew my apple and walnuts at the crest, rifle resting on the spruce log. My bones know they're not here. "They're down there," I say to myself, frustrated at being lured elsewhere, at thinking if I just tried harder, went farther, maybe I would luck on to a new herd.

Coming down the path, I see tracks over my tracks. The fallen aspen compass points directly at a hoof print, freshly squeezed into the dimples where my boots had trod only a couple hours earlier. They were just here. I missed them in my trudging upslope, harder, farther. Trying.

Toward the bottom, deflated and sulking, cow mews and squeals shake my funk. I drop on the spot, set up with the shooting sticks. Although I can't see them, I know they're within thirty-five yards, to the east, in the timbers. Maybe one will step out. I ease the safety off, check the scope, power it down for close-range firing and breathe deeply. The calls persist, as if toying with me, "We've been watching you, woman. Every day. Up and back. Up and back down, you go. We see you." Their banter continues, lightly raising my hopes.

And then nothing. Silence. No movement. Two hours pass, I wait through a couple of remnant calls until I know they've moved on.

The snow from the Wednesday prior has melted in all but the highest places. The tracks of 1,845 elk early on and the bright white of new winter precipitation have faded to a dormant brown. Chances are slim I'll get one, unless I decide to take others' advice and drive the roads. It's illegal to use a vehicle as support when firing. It is also illegal to shoot across any road, so when I see five cows bound from the trees toward a clearing as I round the next corner, I freeze, not knowing what to do.

I hop out, throw my pack on, slam the magazine in the rifle, load and lock the chamber, and head toward the cows. Sunlight trickles from the horizon as I walk the road. There, at thirty yards across the dirt track from me, I catch the shadow of an elk's head out of the corner of my eye. Her wide ears hold still on the other side of the aspen as I tiptoe across the slippery tire tracks. She stands still. With the shooting sticks beneath the rifle, I crouch to my knees and wait for her to turn broadside, revealing the kill zone for a shot. But her turn is complete. Her blonde rump fills the crosshairs as she flies down the hill to meet the others.

Folding the sticks into my pack, I look back before moving. She's there again, just her head peeking out, looking directly up at me. I could take an offhand shot between her eyes at eighty-five yards but lower the .308 instead. Her stare drains the kill from me. Our eye-to-eye gaze lasts long enough for doubt to creep in. I've never taken a head-on shot, and not in the faded light of dusk. I resist the urge to man up.

She descends in silence.

After driving nine miles back to camp, I drive past bearded hunters circled around blazing stone-ringed fire pits, drinks in hand, exchanging smiles and stories. Every morning I'm the first one out and the last one back in the evening along this stretch of campsites. I imagine these guys with multiple elk gutted and hanging at camp. I am a party of one with the one tag that seems increasingly elusive to fill.

I crave home. I want Olivia's sweetness—to hear about school and dance that day, to hear about who she had lunch with and what earrings she chose to match her outfit. I want the almost new moon sky of stars, thick on black, to tell me what to do. The terrestrial tracks lure me from low to high and back. I take a grounded approach, rooted, tangible. Yet still I cannot piece together the necessary variables to make the shot. Could the celestial afford a less rational view? Could the moon-milk light and star gaze shimmer illuminate new clues and ways of seeing?

Tomorrow is my last chance.

Day Six

Wednesday, November 7, 2018. 5:25 a.m. 21 degrees. 99,194 miles. Solitary darkness. No moon.

I pull into the sweet spot at 5:51 a.m. My headlights flash on a red-eyed frenzy of six cows bolting away from the intrusion of my pickup. Shit. That's it. They're gone.

I go through the motions of the pack, the rifle, the shooting sticks tucked under my arm and binos at my neck. I cover the same ground with a few new detours. No elk. No new sign. No calls. No musk. The days before blend into this one, the familiar feeling of waiting, wanting. Midmorning becomes midafternoon. I change direction, my tracks shaping a different path. They have gotten to me. I give up my guard, my tactics, my aim. The animal inside surfaces. She is as real as the elk staring back, shameless.

At the lowest curve in the two-track, pickup in sight, I surrender. I've come full circle, back to the first legal day when the cow had approached me with the aspen at my back. How intimate I am with the rough edge of this opening, the brown-black sludge of the thick clay soil, the elk pellets now dry, faded. I know where the elk have crossed, where they've run for cover, where they've called and bedded down. I drop to the ground, my pack to the side, rifle to the air. There is no more trying, nothing else to do. I know the chances of them coming within range are as slim as the last gasp of sunlight over the western ridge.

I sit. I let them come to me in my mind, my eyes closed—the cows and the bulls, their pungency, their music. I let the thunder of their hooves crossing the road hammer me to the core, bruising their way to my bones. I hear the bull's bugle, rooted in the earth's belly, reach up through his mahogany ankles, into his four-chambered gut, up his thick throat and out his mouth. I let the baritone shake me, my throat, my insides. I breathe him in, absorb his force, crave his power.

Cows meander through my mind, wise in their weaving through

branches, deliberate hooves over undulating meadows. Selective in indulging the bulls' appetite, they know what they want of him, when and how much to take; they know self-preservation. I let them teach me to run wild, to pause, to grip the earth between my toes, poised to nurture new blood, new bones, the next generation. I feel their milk swell in my breasts, their fecund hips spreading as mine did fourteen years ago, their desire to congregate with female solidarity through winter's gestation.

The calf tiptoes into view. I see her coppery hide soft with new life. She trusts her mother's course, her mother's way. Her wet nose, wide, transparent eyes, and velour ears come to attention, mimicking her mother's caution. She prances, delicate collagen toes flutter through my pelvis. I have held her here before in the shelter of my womb. I know the mothering. I know the suckling of young lips at my dripping nipple, the feeding, protecting. I know new life.

I open my eyelids lightly, see the forest motionless. I close my eyes again. Olivia slips in, her legs stretched taut, high. She pirouettes, lips parting to a shy smile just as her neck arches, hair pulled to a neatly coiled bun. She beckons, "Look, Mom, this is called a rond de jambe." Her toes rigid to the floor, I feast on the flight of her spin, the flounce of tights and airy skirt knowing their choreography. She feeds me with her dance, her desire, her eyes wide to the future.

BOOM! My body jerks, eyes bolt open. Someone shoots about five hundred yards to the southeast. Almost last light of the last day; probably the ultimate shot. I imagine it is the thundering of my own rifle at the cow that just happened to step out at the perfect distance, perfect angle from me, where I had been every day prior. Couldn't I be the one with the kill drive taking the shot? I sit, listen for more shots, close my eyes, and let the rifle rest at my side. As the light wanes the bulls stop bugling, and the moon acquiesces.

❦

ON THE NEW moon, the alignment of the earth, sun, and moon is such that the moon is not illuminated by the sun at all and is therefore not visible from earth. Some say it is a time to set intentions, set goals, set off in new directions, fresh starts. The new moon decrescendo of this hunt falls on the last day, the fifth day of the hunt and the sixth day of my time near Cebolla. I find my way in the dark up to the area where the last shot originated. The guys are there, three of them with two pickups, one shining a spotlight onto the ground behind the truck bed.

"You got one, hmmm?" I ask, looking at the gutted carcass of the cow at my feet.

"Yep, just in time. She's not very big but not too small, I guess," the hunter states, flatly.

"She's perfect. Just right." I mutter. "How did you do it?"

"We had been hunting over near Canjilon the whole time but all the elk we saw were at least one thousand yards away. Too far to shoot. So we decided to try it over here this last evening. Saw her running and then I used this." He holds up the neon-green cow call hanging from the black string around his neck. "Got her to stop just long enough."

She lays on her right side, abdomen concave, stomach, intestines, and vital organs in a steaming heap a few feet away, bloody flesh flapping open where the knife split her from her anus to her breastbone.

She lies precisely at the spot I had parked my first day, fifteen feet from the road.

I congratulate the guys, making my way back down to the pickup as they prepare the winch whose coarse cable will tug her by the ankles into their truck, returning with her to camp to join the others in their group who have already tagged out.

After a numb ride back to camp, the Airstream awaits, like a silver ghost in my headlights. In the past, the last nights of the hunt have been full of clinking wine glasses, loaded plates of local café enchiladas, and the telling and retelling of every moment of the hunt and the kill. Al and I would celebrate plenty as we ate and then later, when our bodies found each other, inflamed and exhausted, fling fleece vests to the ground, tug woolen sweaters overhead, and pull down long johns. His bulky hands would stretch the two-inch section of cotton crotch panty to the side just enough to make accessible what had been confined all day. We feasted.

I pull in front of the camper, back into position near the hitch, turn the engine off, and sit silently. While the dogs yelp below, I trace constellations above—Orion, Pleiades, the Big Dipper—seeing them more clearly with peripheral vision. The elk come to me this way, too, when my focus loosens. How far away is Orion's belt, the Seven Sisters in their twinkling frolic, the North Star? What fades in the four years it takes the light of the closest star to reach our eyes? How far from the road was the man when he took the shot? How long would it have taken my .308 bullet to penetrate her hide, blast her heart and lungs into a mangled mass? If I had taken the shot on opening evening, how long would it have been until the cow fell to the ground with only her calf and me to witness the final flutter of hooves, the death spasms? What split-second choices have I made that make or take life? What do I have to show for them?

"I didn't get one, honey," I confess to Olivia through the phone, trying to deaden my voice. Silence. "It's OK, Mom. You were so close to them. Every day. You can come home now."

❦

I PACK THE coolers, load and strap down supplies in the pickup bed, and drag my feet to make the trip back to town. The rifle rests unused in the back seat. The five blue-tipped bullets remain packed in the magazine laying in the console by my cell phone. The game bags are clean, gauzy white in the pack, and knives shine tidy. I have no blood beneath my nails, no ache in my back from hauling meat. The butchering counter will be barren, plates empty. I have nothing to bring home.

Miles click rapidly on the odometer over asphalt. My body no longer moves slowly by foot, but my bones, my gut, are still there with the elk.

They come to me as I drive, softening my view. Unafraid, they move in closer. The food that was mine to take by trigger, to offer once I had returned home as a celebrated hunter, remains hoofed, finding night and day by scent and sound. I let them feed me now, fill my desire, render me new.

The moon exhales, empty, unapologetic. How long until snow falls again to obscure the outline of old imprints and reveal paths of fresh tracks? Where will the elk be tomorrow? Will they see the dimples from my hooves, smell my yellow stains?

How do I resuscitate the dream as it wanes upon waking, snatched away from my grasp when I open my eyes?

WAXING

First appearance of the moon after the invisible phase.

She is only partially illuminated by the sun, young still.

DREAM STAGES

Non-Rapid Eye Movement (NREM) sleep when dreams do not occur.

Decreased blood flow to brain and muscle.

Believed to be the majority of overall sleep experience.

2010–2017

SHOOT LIKE A GIRL

MY BELLY ON VERMEJO ground, a small herd of elk downhill and upwind, I have a solid opportunity. Lying at my side with binos in hand, Al encourages, "You got it, babe. Go for it."

I've never taken a shot at a big animal. This is my first.

"You sure? They're so far . . . Can I make the shot?" I steady my focus, slow my breath, and eliminate all internal and external distractions. The taking of this elk's life cannot be cluttered with self-doubt and what-ifs. Wind and shifting light may alter visibility, but I remain resolute.

BAM! The rifle fire splits the morning open. Mid-chew, the elk lifts her head, pauses, then teeters and spins once counterclockwise.

She folds to the earth.

❦

THE 590,823-ACRE Vermejo Ranch owned by Ted Turner is situated just west of Raton, between the eastern Great Plains of northern New Mexico and the Sangre de Cristo mountains at the lower end of the Rockies. The ranch offers hunting, fishing, and outdoor recreation opportunities and is also managed for habitat and wildlife conservation. Most of the ranch is drained by the Canadian River and its tributary Vermejo Creek. Some of the western portion of the ranch flows west to the Rio Grande.

There are approximately ten thousand elk, three thousand mule deer, and two thousand bison, as well as pronghorn antelope, Rocky Mountain bighorn sheep, black bears, mountain lions, and Merriam's turkeys, a subspecies of the wild turkey, on the ranch.

This is an animal's paradise. A hunter's, too.

❧

"WAIT. JUST WAIT. You're not going anywhere near that elk for at least an hour, Christie," Al snaps during this first elk hunt on the Vermejo. My shot with Al's 7 mm had penetrated some part of the animal's body but, at over two hundred yards we can't tell where the bullet hit.

"She's not going anywhere unless we barge over there. Then the adrenaline will kick in and we'll never track her down. Come on, let's go have breakfast."

We walk the half mile back to the pickup, climb in the cab and pass each other handfuls of mixed nuts, gooey green chile breakfast burrito bites, and sour apple wedges. I understand the seriousness of the situation and Al's firm instruction. But I'm eager.

"How 'bout now? Can't we go now?" Worry kneads my gut, pounds in my head. What if she's gone? What if I blew my first kill in a "blood and done" deflation.

❧

"BLOOD AND DONE" is the philosophy of this private ranch, meaning if you wound an animal and the animal gets away, your hunt is over. The hunting and fishing lodge on the Stony River west of the Alaska Range had the same rule. I worked summers there as a pastry chef, butchered game animals and fleshed their hides to fund my UC Berkeley college education.

I kneaded bread dough for dinner, rolled out pie crusts, and dished up the sweet of each meal for lodge guests and the crew. My role was relegated to *staff,* a behind-the-scenes worker humming the lodge along, tidy, efficient. I envied the glamour of the guides and pilots, the men with the know-how in the air, on foot, and in the rivers, the men with the wilds at their fingertips. I served with a smile but secretly craved venturing beyond log wall confines. One evening, when I presented the platter of steaming moose roast to the table of men, a guest smirked, "What's for supper tonight? Caribou steak? Salmon fillet? Or inner thigh of a Berkeley junior?" Biting my tongue, I centered the food on the table. The rest of the crew and the lodge owner sat, silent. Could a pack on my back and rifle in hand have elevated my status, freed me from the tidily tied apron and feigned acceptance of the too-small, good-girl role?

As the fishing season transitioned into hunting, my hands made more than pleasing pastries. Holding moose, caribou, Dall sheep, and bear in my palms, I learned these animals firsthand. Their flesh in mine, their faces turned inside out with each stroke of my knife, I absorbed the scent, textures, and weight of their bodies. Eyelashes, lips, tongues, and fur—I was afforded rare proximity with the animals of Alaska I had feared and revered as a child growing up in Anchorage. Then they were larger than me, larger than life. Now they were literally in my lap. As they became intimate kin, I was less able to see them as other. While I peeled hide and muscle from the curved claws and knuckled joints of the bear's paw, my five fingers pressed into hers, nearly identical.

Some of the hunters at the Stony sauntered around taking sloppy shots, aiming at the animals as if they existed for the men's sake, for their entertainment and consumption, posing like heroes for the trophy photograph even when it was the guide who made the lethal shot. Once, back after dark from tracking a wounded black bear, a guest at the lodge had pressed the guide. "Let's go again tomorrow. First thing. I know I can take one with the next shot. I know I'll hit it." They had tracked the bear up the craggy slope behind camp for the better part of the evening after the hunter had missed the kill zone, likely hitting the gut instead of the vital organs. Spots of blood on alder leaves, cow parsnip, and spongy tundra lead them higher and higher, but not to the bear.

Secretly I imagined the bear making her escape with only a superficial wound. I saw her alighting upslope through dense brush, far beyond the range of the greedy hunter.

❦

AFTER THE LONGEST hour, Al and I make our way back to the shooting spot in silence. I see her through the binos about twenty-five yards from where she fell, legs tucked beneath her, head up.

"You need to shoot her again."

Assuming my prone position, pack at rifle rest, I take aim at the base of her neck, thankful her eyes look the other way. The weight of the moment stifles. Ponderosas stand still. Birds cease to chirp. Even the ravens stop teasing.

WHAM! Her head snaps sideways, body melts to the earth. No breath. No movement. Final surrender.

❦

WE ROLL THE elk to her back and see the penis at the soft, blond belly. "A bull. It's a bull." The tag allows one antlerless elk, so it's a legal kill. This bull is likely a yearling, still in the care of its mother alongside other cows and their calves. I roll the cuffs of Al's Pendleton up to his elbows, unscrew the Nalgene lid, rinse the knife. With skinning knife at the bull's head, I extract the blossomed copper bullet from the right nostril.

The neck shot blew straight through, lodging the bullet into squishy nose flesh. I pull it out and place it in my back pocket.

❦

THEY SAY WOMEN are better shots than men. That women take

their time, are more careful. Years after that kill, over dinner after a hunt in which I hadn't brought home an elk, I describe to guests the swirling wind, the blizzard, the questioning of conditions as I lie, finger on trigger, crosshairs positioned on restless elk, with Al flaring, "Just shoot!" The young bulls were in front of my target, and the cow changed direction and position at least three times. Then shifting wind blew our cover and off they ran. I lost my chance at that first shot of the hunt.

Hunters have even been categorized into types, not just by gender (95 percent are men, even though the percentage of female hunters has more than doubled since the eighties), but by philosophy. Stephen Kellert categorizes hunters as one of three types: utilitarian/meat hunters; dominionistic/sport hunters; and nature hunters. Marti Kheel classifies us as either happy, holistic, or holy.

Back at the Stony River Lodge as a college student unbridled in the Alaska wilds, happy, holistic, and holy never crossed my mind. Charged with squirrel duty, an assignment of new empowerment I happily accepted, outfitted with a 12 gauge, and twenty years old, I shot the jittery, squeaking critters offhand without hesitation. Opportunists, they invaded the canvas wall tent pantry daily. My ears, conditioned to their perky chatter, cued me to grab the gun, run to them and shoot. Their bodies dropped from spruce limbs to the ground, a soft thud followed by several flailing flops, sudden stiffened hind legs, and a last, shuddered gasp. I scooped up the limp bodies into a rusty shovel, carrying them to the river to let the Stony current carry the corpses away. I didn't know I'd be shooting, skinning, and eating squirrels as part of my hunting practice twenty-five years later.

"Shoot straight. Make it count. Ammo's expensive, Christie," lodge owner Jim admonished.

❦

AFTER WE'VE GUTTED, quartered, and bagged the elk, with Al

doing most of the work and showing me how to make each cut, we leave the gut pile behind for scavengers, and drive back to the Whittington Center just south of Raton near the Colorado state line. We hang the quarters from the porch just outside our room. We're not members of the NRA but choose to stay here for relatively easy access to the Vermejo. We like the simple dorm-style accommodations and kitchens with enough cooking supplies to serve up warm meals at night.

With the meat hung and the sun set, we transition indoors to unwind, feast and celebrate. Al warms flour tortillas on the stove flame, then butters and folds them into quarters. I stir the ice chunk from the middle of the red chile posole we had pulled from the freezer at home for easy heat-and-eat meals here.

"That felt so far, Al. That was a long shot." I say, blowing into the stew on my spoon.

"Yeah, it was a little far for your first shot but not too far. You had a good rest. You did a good job." Al smiles, tearing open a tortilla oozing with butter. His lips shine and beard glistens.

❦

I HAD WONDERED if I could hunt too. If I could add to my experience and desire for locally harvested food. I had gardened. I had fished and been around hunting, but had never taken the first step to learn, to go for it, until Al showed up. But there was a different itch, something pulling me toward the hunt beyond the pursuit of food and self-reliance.

With the dissolution of the El Guique dream and the goodbye to that land, the Rio Grande, the San Rafael del Guique acequia, Olivia and I grew into our Santa Fe home. An ember still smoldered inside. A different, expanded dream took hold.

I wanted what the men had: free range.

Olivia's father came and went. Al popped in on the winds of whim.

Kissing Al goodbye without knowing the timing of his return, longing for the presence of a father for Olivia, and bagging up tasty lunches and wishing the hunters good luck on their outings as a young woman all fueled the cumulative fire of rebellion inside. Now, at age thirty-eight, I wondered, why couldn't I get what I wanted too? And could the getting be in direct defiance of the casual taking? Could I do it differently? Could I roam, hunt, and make food and life on my terms, unrestrained? Through the hunt and through a detached relationship with Al, could I do what women aren't supposed to: put my pleasure, my way first?

❦

AFTER DISHES, WITH satiated bellies and showered bodies, Al pulls me close. We've fashioned a bed on the floor from the dorm-style twin mattresses. Flannel sheets, wool blankets, and a down comforter, four fluffed pillows and my cashmere shawl cradle our rocking bodies. Al had forgotten to take off his head lamp. We laughed as he dialed it to its red light setting for fun, coloring our sex hot. His calloused hands roll my hips over, belly to the floor. He raises my hips high, climbs behind. My hair falls over my lowered head, my hands clutch his fingers, my nose inhales the blood crusted on his cuticles. Couldn't this last forever, this loosening of laws that I followed so diligently at home between the four walls of profession and domesticity? The wild ignited an animal inside me that hadn't been allowed to wander, to wonder, to respond to bodily calls in new directions, toward new scents. Al liked me wild here too.

I didn't know twenty-three years ago when I first met him at Janell and Byron's wedding in North Dakota that he'd be here with me like this now. I had been asking for "six foot three and good hands" for years. When Al, tall, weathered, and able, walked into my life again, I hadn't been with a man—not even a hug or hand hold—since before Olivia's birth four years earlier. My body was ready to make up for the dry spell.

❦

WHEN AL CAME to me in Santa Fe in 2008 when the chicken coop needed his hammer and nails for completion, he said, "Pleased to meet you, Christie Green. Again." I had to look away from his humble smile and sandy hair tucked beneath a stained camo cap. The twinkle of his pale blue eyes—one flecked with brown—pierced me through. Our hands lingered, palm to palm, mine dwarfed in his massive mitt. We stood still, taking us in.

Glancing down at my red Birkenstock garden clogs, Al asked, "Should I take my boots off?"

"Nah, this floor hasn't been cleaned in months. What's another set of tracks?" I called back, head turned toward the kitchen, full of blush and a tingling in my belly that I thought had atrophied.

"We're having fajitas tonight. I just got home from pruning a client's fruit trees. This will be quick. Are you hungry?" I had no clue about Al's appetite then. That his belly was never full, his hunger never satisfied. I didn't know enough to take small bites then, to savor one course at a time with him, that eating too much, too fast, might push us past reason.

"You bet!" he affirmed. "I'm ready when you are."

"Come on, Olivia, sweetie. Wash your hands. Let's eat, hon," I shout back to Olivia in her room. I hadn't introduced Olivia to any previous suitors, even those wanting a first date to include her. I knew better than to expose what was most valued, most vulnerable. Maybe this man was a safer bet, being an impossible match. With Al's intermittent passing through, neither I nor Olivia could collapse toward him.

She pads out on three-year-old feet, crayon in her right fist, and peeks at Al from behind the wisp of silky hair falling around her wide eyes. She races back to the bathroom to climb up on the step stool to reach the sink.

"Honey, this is Al. He's going to visit for a few days, going to help with the chicken coop." My cheery introduction camouflaged the inkling of dread inside. I knew what happened with the last man who came to help.

Olivia pulls out the porcelain doll our friend Marlyn had sent for Christmas and hands it to Al. The shattered face lands in his palm, tiny pieces rattling inside the hollow head. "See my doll?" she asks, looking up at him. "She's all broke!" Olivia says, matter of fact.

"Well, I can glue her up good as new after supper if you like," Al offers.

Olivia pulls herself to her chair and fondles the steamy flour tortilla wrapped around the sautéed peppers, onions, and beef. She smears sour cream in swirls on her plate and uses her chubby flat palms to pull the sippy cup to her lips, sucking the apple juice in.

Al fixes the next night's supper of flash sautéed scaled quail from his most recent hunt down near Silver City, New Mexico. As he chews he reaches up to the shelf over the dining table to the dried corkscrew *Stipa neomexicana* grass seed head, and asks, "You ever seen this?" Pulling the seed to his mouth, he sticks his tongue out and wets the tip of the seed. "Watch."

Set on the tabletop, the seeds slowly spins, trying to penetrate the hard surface, pushing itself as DNA instructs toward what it hopes is fertile propagation ground.

"Isn't that so cool?" Al smiles, "Those grasses know how to get through hard desert ground. Just like that, with the slightest moisture, they drill themselves in."

I can hardly respond, my heart swelling with all we have in common. He's from the land, too, a prairie farm boy who knows baling wire and duct tape. His hands make, know how to repair what's broken.

"Pappa will like him," I think to myself.

Over the course of the next three days, Al opens me to new flavors, hydrates all that's parched. My body comes to life.

"Why don't you stick around awhile?" I teased.

In the morning after his first night in our guest casita, he cradles his English Setters, Riggs and Jenny, with long, muscled arms, extracts them from the funky silver dog trailer behind the diesel Ford and sets them down on the gravel driveway.

"Where can I stake these two out, Christie? Got a patch of grass anywhere?"

❦

BACK HOME AFTER my first elk hunt at the Vermejo, we begin to cut. I hold the young bull's hind quarter up alongside me. With his ankle in my hand, toes pointing up, the slippery ball joint of his femur extends nearly to my foot. After Al snaps a photo, I lay the leg on the kitchen counter atop clean white butcher paper secured with masking tape. Knives and cutting boards at hand, I glide my fingers inside muscle groups, separate clusters of thick fat, stretching sinew and fascia to slice newly defined portions that will feed us.

My body touching the elk's body, I slip into heightened awareness of my own glutes, quadriceps, and complex musculature of forearms and calves where fine, splintery bones and tendons comprise this essential corporal architecture. These muscles burn, ascending me up slopes to long ridges, holding me steady as I descend the other side. Am I, too, animal armature?

"One hundred and eight pounds," Al declares, holding the tidy, rectangular butcher paper packages with black Sharpie labels—Chops, Steak, Burger—in a bundle over the scale. The marrow-rich legs have been bent at the joints curving over the picket fence to the east, drying in the sun before being cut into dog bones. "Plenty to stock the freezer until next fall's hunt," Al smiles.

The butchering complete and a year's worth of meat tucked in the freezer, I relax into bed, Al snoring beside me. We transition back into the straight-line world within the confines of walls, with the shrill signal of the alarm clock setting the scheduled pace of the day and the ambient roar of vehicles on the grid of roads. Against these "real world" elements, the elk flesh on my fingers fades, the elk scent in my nostrils is neutralized.

I beg for the dream to pull me under, to return me.

My feet are bare. I'm in my place: the mountains where the elk, deer, turkeys, bears, cougars, ravens, and non-humans fly, crawl, strut, and run. I can be free here, too, like them.

I ride the fifty-dollar, 1990s-yard-sale mountain bike with clanging sprocket and rusty chain along the fence line heading east just past the alpine meadow. Dawn light teases new shadows beneath the ponderosa. I wonder who's watching me.

As I peddle I hear an elk bugling to the north. How could it be? This is not the elk mating season. Does the bull know how badly I want him? Does he know my cycle is monthly, not yearly. I'm here. Coming closer.

Circling slowly, doubling back on my route, I lag to a careful crawl. I listen through my pores. He bugles again, his belly and throat opening wider. His thick hooves rumble the roots, moving in my direction. The bull penetrates the space, cracking open the sleepy mountains, lakes, and canyons.

I smile wide at his gift. His taunting. If only he knew.

I put my bare feet square to the ground, straddle the bike, inhale the bull.

At dawn's liminal edge, the shot fires in my ears, the memory of the trigger pulls my index finger toward my heart. I wonder if that was the best I could do.

❦

HAPPY, HOLISTIC OR holy? I had asked Al to teach me to hunt within a year of our fajita supper, probably one of the last meals of beef my household has tasted. Why not learn to harvest my own meat? It seemed a natural complement to all of the food I was growing at home for Olivia and me, and for clients on their land.

"Babe, what would you think of taking me hunting? I think I want to try big game." I pondered the possibility with Al.

"Well, hell yes!" he bolted upright, setting his hunting magazine on the arm of the chair. "We should go shoot, get you set up with a rifle. It's too late to put in for the public land hunt this year, but I bet we could find a late-season cow tag on private land. I'll look online."

Al supported my desire to hunt, as if my learning fed his own passion. He got to see the tracking, the animals, even their guts and hooves anew. "Babe, I've never been with anyone who takes as many pictures as you do. Never seen anyone photograph gut piles, my hands in the belly, the skulls boiling on the stove," he observed.

"Come here," he'd say, opening his long arms to me, enfolding my trembles in the comfort of the warm wool. "Hold still. The cutting can wait a minute." I was always torn after making the kill. Had I done it right? Was the trigger pulled with intention? Did I shoot like a girl, like the "girly" fishing I had done alongside my brother and father on the Kenai River in Alaska when their hands yanked the slippery salmon egg bait from me with impatient frowns?

My dad had headed north to Alaska at the direction of the Army, but also inspired by his own hunting and fishing desires. Pappa chose to farm, to plow the Plains. He chose an unbridled lifestyle, being his own boss even while at the mercy of weather and wheat prices. My brother claimed himself as a fisheries biologist; he was born practically part fish, a baited hook in his hand nearly before he could walk.

What reason would be good enough for me—a woman—to choose the unlikely El Guique farm to work and water? To choose the man with copper bracelets? To land on the six-foot-three tall man with good hands who was only there to finish off the chicken coop?

How did I choose Olivia, or did she choose me? And the mothering?

The undercurrent of questions like, "Who do you think you are?" and connotations such as, "*That* kind of woman," still tugged at the hem of my skirt. Can I be all woman and choose how much of the manly in me I want to embolden?

Have I been happy, holistic, or holy in my choices? Or am I like them, the seeds, the river current, the animals who find their way downstream, migrate over mountains, blow in the wind to their destination of open ground, penetrating the soil with just enough moisture at just the right time?

THIRTY-SIX WEEKS

"IT'S ONE O'CLOCK. LET'S take a nap. The elk won't be active now anyway." Al and I pull over on the two-track dirt road northwest of Springer, New Mexico, in Game Management Unit 56, a region south of the New Mexico-Colorado border, in the valley of the Cimarron River, six miles west of the Cimarron-Canadian River confluence where Rocky Mountain foothills transition into grassy plains. The low, mid-January sun beckons us to lie still, calm like the dormant, straw-colored grass, to rest while we can after having been up in search of elk for eight hours already.

"No elk here. We haven't seen elk for two years. Too dry." All the local landowners whose doors we knock on say the same thing. Our chances are pretty much slim to none on this hunt, but we persist even after sitting the first day from sunup to sundown behind our makeshift camouflage blind above a dusty, shallow arroyo, waiting and watching for elk who never came. No sign. No tracks, as if the dry riverbed were skeletal remains of the water that once flowed its course, and of the elk who ascended its banks to cross to grassier south-facing slopes.

Our second night in town, while savoring green chile enchiladas topped with pungent white onions and greasy sopaipillas laced with sticky honey at the local diner, we asked others if they knew where we might find any elk on any ranch owner's land. This was a unit-wide rather than ranch-only hunt: the entire unit, including private and public land, was open to us, though we needed written permission for private access.

Today is our lucky day. Tony, from Raton, answers the phone at noon when we call to ask permission. "We heard you might have elk on your land. Could we give it a go?" He agrees to drive the hour to meet us, show us his property boundaries, and point out any likely spots the elk could be grazing or migrating through.

While waiting for Tony, I eke out a high spot with faint cell reception to call Olivia, who's staying with her "auntie," Patty. "Hi, Mom. Did you get one yet?" After a quick catch-up and news of our cat, Edmund, and his latest rabbit kill, we say "I love you" and hang up. Al and I curl up in the thick gold, rust, and brown afghan my grandmother had crocheted tucked around us in the pickup bed. I settle into this time, into Al, as welcome respite from the schedules and responsibilities of town. Here I'm allowed to slough logic. The sun eases our weary bodies as we lie together and lazily explore each other's shapes beneath the covers, hands on camo pants and shirts, feeling the soft and hard places. The rough palms of Al's hands snag the fine silk fabric of my long john undershirt. We're too tired to roll into full lovemaking this afternoon; we'll get to that tonight in a motel room lit by the blinking "no vacancy" sign.

I plunge toward silent darkness, fatigue tugging me under. The days are long, nights short. Dreams are pinched by the morning alarm. Today, with the warmth of Al, enrobed in comfortable respite, I allow the previous night's images to surface. Something disturbing confronted me face-to-face, nose-to-nose. Her eyes penetrated, though I couldn't make out her form. Her scent lingered thick at my throat. In the immediacy of her presence I'm unable to swallow or breathe. A scream punctures me.

I wake to the sound of truck tires approaching on the chalky gravel road. "Hi! Are you Tony?" Indeed, it's him. I try to shake the bone-deep chill of the daydream, force a cordial greeting, and extend my hand to our host.

With bright eyes and a faintly discernible smile, his face is all but gone from the nose down. It's hard to shift my stare from what looks like multiple massive face reconstructions, plastic surgeries, and skin grafts to piece back together what were his lips, chin, mouth, and throat. We get to talking elk as he hops in the cab to show us fence lines and boundaries.

Not two minutes later Al and I point. "Look there, up on the slope . . . *elk*!"

"No, those are horses," Tony says.

"Nope, those for sure are elk." Al shifts the pickup into reverse, slowly backing up to the curvy section we can park along to be obscured from the grazing animals. Adrenaline fuels me into swift motion to heft my pack, sling binos over my neck, grab and load the 7mm—safety on—and tread up the grassy hill. Tony agrees to wait and watch from the far hill while I make the stalk.

This is my fourth elk hunt in as many years. The first two were successful; the third, a bow hunt, wasn't. We know how sparse the elk are in this unit and it's been a year since I've stocked the freezer. I rush to the shooting position, awkward with the massive 7mm slung over my shoulder. It's not my gun; it's Al's, and more suited for his long arms which easily have six inches on mine. But the bolt-action rifle, looking and feeling more like an assault machine, is what I've shot before, positioned over the sandbag rest on the shooting bench, aiming at a bull's-eyes one hundred to three hundred yards away.

Although I imagine owning a rifle of my own someday, one that more closely conforms to my shape and size like an extension of my hands and arms, this one will have to do. Ravens glide on shifting wind, the direction of our scent at its mercy.

We crest the hill. Spot seven cows, no bulls. The cows have moved away from the pesky, juvenile satellite bulls and domineering herd bulls that wrangle them during the mating cycle rut of autumn. Although the cows and bulls may remain together for weeks, mating numerous times, the cows' estrus cycles last only a few days. Now their relaxed meander in grazing and resting on the shady slope implies casual calm as they satisfy their daily twenty-pound intake of grass, forbs, and bark. But I know one hint of human scent will blow our cover. I lower myself to my belly and use my forearms to crawl up the curve of the hill, tufts of grass pushed flat beneath my weight. An occasional prickly cactus spine tugs at my pants. *Artemisia frigida* releases its pungent counterpoint to winter's cool with each lug of my inner thighs pumping up the incline. Stopping to glass, I assess the position of the elk and check to see if we've been busted. So far, so good.

I halt just before the slope levels. Al is ten feet behind me. I position my backpack ahead, laying it flat to serve as my rifle rest. This is the steadiest way to take a shot. Less room for error from a wavering rifle because of nerves and wobbly legs or rickety shooting sticks positioned on uneven ground. I like to shoot lying down, my body in full contact with the ground beneath me. Solid, supported, I watch and wait. All the elk are either lying down or hidden behind piñon or one-seed juniper trees. Finally, after what feels like an extended pause, one rises and nonchalantly makes her way down the slope to what must have looked like especially tasty grass; she's set on her destination.

There she stands, head behind the conifer, body fully broadside. I fidget, impatient. I make one last assessment of distance with the range finder, inhaling calm, steadying my hands—one with its forefinger on the trigger, the other resting on top of the rifle. With my crosshairs centered on the kill zone, I squeeze, sending the bullet the 156 yards through her thick hide, penetrating her heart and lungs, then exiting through her other side.

Her front right leg crumbles beneath her, a grotesque contortion of downward momentum tumbling her to the steep ravine. Clumps of intermittent juniper trunks slow her mass. I wait, watch her fall, wonder if she'll get back up as injured animals often do, fueled by their own survival adrenaline. She lies still. Al and I approach slowly, making our way down the hillside, across the ravine, and up the slope she grazed without taking our eyes off her slumped body, my rifle at the ready. My hands tremble: grief and elation course their conflicting juices through my cells. Another life taken. I push my booted foot into the thick of her hip, crouch down, touch her broad belly, look at her glassy brown eye. Eyelashes long and gentle remain at attention, lining open lids.

"Let me have some time with her," I say to Al.

"Sure, I'll just go get the pickup," he responds, his fingers gliding along mine. He lifts my pinky slightly from beneath as if trying to aerate my heaviness. I trace my hands along her muscled flanks, sinewy forelegs, plush white belly, and bend my nose to her hide, inhaling every inch of the body that will soon become the material of muscle that feeds us. My hands move along her curves, hips, shoulders, solid rump, and coarse, worn hooves. Her ears are soft to the touch but stiff, as if supported inside by a puppeteer's hand that holds them erect against the tug of death's gravity. Her chin prickles with whiskers—grass still clenched between her teeth. A lazy lip sags to the soil. Her crimson blood coagulates into thick pudding puddles.

Sensing movement from her lower belly, I see her auburn hide punch up and then sink down, as if something larger than bowels is moving within. The dread in my belly confirms the grim truth. The baby elk inside must have been conceived during the rut just four months prior. Like other elk in the region, this one would have been born in mid- to late May after a thirty-six-week gestation period, depending on weather conditions. Like newborn humans, this elk would have latched on to its mother's milk for immediate nourishment.

None of the other cow elk I have killed bore fetuses. Today my shot took a second life. I sit alongside her fading warmth, fascinated by the life holding on inside as her body stiffens. Then I go numb. Twelve years earlier, I'd borne a fetus, a life inside my own body that was never birthed.

❦

THE FATHER WAS a neighbor I'd been spending time with since settling into the El Guique homestead a year or so earlier and a few years before I met Olivia's father. He invited me to work cattle in the high country during the summer months. I helped train his new colt, going round and round at rope's end in the corral, sharing stories all the while of sowing seeds, acequia irrigation, and the famous red chile grown for generations by his Hispanic family.

I needed someone to show me the way here in northern New Mexico, a place so different from Alaska and different, too, from the 640-acre sections of wheat my Pappa farmed in Texas. I imagined my time with the cowboy who befriended me in a neighborly way could somehow resuscitate and recreate the stability of a home and place I could count on—just like my Pappa's homestead where he had broken ground, raised a family, and farmed for forty years. I tried to root myself in the land, soil, and water, in the strength of generations passing along rituals of food, lore, harvest and harmony. I resisted settling for anything akin to what my parents endured in their marriage, their isolation thousands of miles away in Alaska.

Mom met my proclamation of pregnancy with a deflated, blank stare. She loved having grandchildren (my brother had two kids already), but she didn't want mine to come this way, as a surprise, out of wedlock. She finally eased, conceding, "You never do follow the rules or do things in the right order. I guess this time is no different."

My body changed, my nipples tingled, and as I read every night about the growing life inside me, I knew this was a kind of calling. The father was less excited, having raised two kids of his own already and gone through a rough divorce. His eyes were set on the near horizon of retirement, not changing diapers.

Although we tried to maintain our friendship and continue with regular contact, I noticed his increasing distance. "I'll be rounding up the herd tonight. Gotta get them in off the mesa." I knew he was checking out and would likely become completely unavailable once the baby was born. I was two months pregnant: could I raise a child on my own? How would the baby and I be received in this all-Catholic community, where family ties are strong and loyalty deep? I'm white, and we we're not married. I'm not from here.

In the second month, as the pregnancy became more real, he asserted his soon-to-be fatherhood: "There's no way I'm going to let some woman tell me what I can or can't do with my own kid like my first wife did. I'm damn sure going to take this kid and do what I want, when I want." My stomach tightened, the steely reality of division settling in.

Two days later, while we were driving through town on a warm July evening, a cold distance separated us on the front seat of his diesel pickup. I noticed people strolling on sidewalks and through shady parks with roadside sunflowers in bloom. A group of women, wearing fanny packs with water bottles and donning summery shorts and tank tops, crossed in front of us as he pulled to a stop to let them pass.

He and I had been out with the horses that day and were heading home. Early in my pregnancy I felt swollen with my desire to mother, to birth, and to nurture. But a deeper doubt tugged within. Was this the man with whom I wanted to share parenting? Would he be an equal partner? I wanted the idyllic summer surroundings to reassure me of a sunny future.

But just as the women walked by, he quipped, "And they wonder why they get raped."

We rode the remaining thirty minutes in silence. He dropped me at the cattle guard at the top of my driveway and waved a nonchalant goodbye as I headed over the acequia bridge to my front door.

❦

AL RETURNS; TONY follows in the quad with bulky chains in tow. I sit, unable to speak as they wind the chains around the elk's rear legs. We're high on the slope. It's getting dark. Butchering and packing will last beyond sunset into the clear night's chill, and we'll still have a two-hour drive ahead to the hotel. I reluctantly agree to let them wrap the chains around her ankles, condemning elegance to indignity.

With each tug of the chain around her ankles, I feel a corresponding tug in my own body as the elk thumps down the hill. I see again the poster of a fuzzy bunny overhead in the abortion clinic, strategically placed as a soft distraction. I wish I had pushed the doctor aside and held my own fetus, my own tiny life in the making. I wish I had pushed away my shyness at asking the unaskable: May I hold my dead baby? May I know its sex? May I feel its barely formed, webbed feet and hands? May I know, even for a brief moment, what this life that has grown inside me looks like?

I follow the elk, knowing by now the life inside her has stopped trying to live off her mother's remnant pulse. A reckoning is imminent as my buck knife plunges deeply into her belly, penetrating sternum to anus. With the knife's puncture, the tight hide stretched over her muscled armature gives way to a sharp spew of gut air. With my sleeves scrunched up beyond elbows' bend—fabric already spotted with warm blood—I reach, shoulder-deep, to cut at the tough diaphragm membrane holding her innards neatly in place. My head contorts above her sternum, soft hide tickling my chin, as I strain to lengthen my reach while my fingers and knife tip see what my eyes cannot. With small, precise slices, I sever the diaphragm's hold, push back up off my knees, widen my arms to engulf the gut mass. I wedge both hands beneath the leaden, two-foot diameter grass-swollen stomach, hoisting entrails to the ground. Her guts are about a third of my weight, every pound resisting my clumsy tugs. Almost falling toward the spilled momentum, I regain balance, composing the knife for more cuts.

I circle the anus surgically so as not to puncture the intestine and release fecal pellets that could contaminate the meat. I re-enter the cavity, now sloshing with quarts of blue-black blood, retrieve the disparate bits of whitish pink lung. I cut between hard ridges of two-inch diameter windpipe and esophagus, yanking tendons that inadvertently nod her throat and chin toward me. Unrecognizable as the once-vital organ, her heart sinks into the arced rib cage.

We butcher, Al and I, into the night. Tony has long since departed after bloody handshakes, a couple hundred dollars of thanks, and goodbye. Al lugs one hindquarter in a bloodstained gauze game bag to the pickup bed, loading what was our sweet nap spot just hours earlier full of meat. As he walks away, his wool-jacketed back to me, I seek out the fetus, the sack of life among guts, there, beyond my right hand's reach. I inch closer, squinting my eyes, trying to discern the details. My fingertips acquaint themselves with the delicate luminescence, a hazy blue-white-pink beneath a transparent uterine skein. Tiny fully formed collagen hooves, knobby knees and elbows, a faint, still head. I wish again that I had sat up then, reached down between my bent thighs and held my baby—known its sex, shape, slippery weight in my hands.

Al returns after loading the pickup. He looks at the fetal sac. "Is that what I think it is?" he asks. I don't answer. My limbs, heavy with labor, linger over the fetus and guts we will leave behind for coyotes, ravens, hawks, and other opportunists to scavenge.

The weight of the silence on the windy road back to the interstate and hotel mutes any inclination to celebrate. The details of today's kill stick in my throat, too heavy to swallow. No glass of wine or fancy dinner to cheer our success.

Al unlocks the door. Once inside I peel off sweaty layers, liberate my ponytail, step in the shower, turning the water up—hot. I see Tony's face and wonder if he feels this way each time he sees his reflection in the mirror? When the gun barrel was snug beneath his chin, just before pulling the trigger, did he worry others would judge the choice he made as a sin rather than a right to relief from suffering? Was his gun meant to be a steward of death? An angel of mercy? Was he thankful the gun didn't go off correctly—the bullet penetrating bone, flesh, and muscle but not enough of what's vital inside to be lethal? With his voice now altered as severely as his face—forcing listeners to inch closer to decipher sounds as mangled as the form from which they flow—is he reminded with each word he speaks that he once chose death? Can he explain?

I crawl into bed next to Al, body flushed. I have killed. I have birthed. I reach for Al's rough hands, place them on my curves beneath the blankets. His solid touch, hushed voice, heavy thighs between mine console. I let him absorb many truths from my body.

He whispers, "You did a good job. She's beautiful. We'll cut meat this week. We'll feast and share."

Olivia comes to mind as I drift off to sleep, "It's OK, Mom, I'm here. I can't wait until you come home. I want to see you. And the elk."

No dreams tonight. Just the elk at my fingertips.

$1.67

I SIT AT THE oval-shaped conference table with the men. Some call me a landscaper, some a landscape designer, while others call me a landscape architect, a title I'm allowed to claim since I have an advanced degree, have passed four national exams that cost $350-$550 each, and have satisfied licensure application requirements. This title validates me as someone designing for "the health and safety" of the public. I can charge a higher hourly rate and put three letters behind my name: PLA, Professional Landscape Architect.

In the conference room the developer blasts, "I can't stand edibles, Christie. And fruit trees. I *hate* fruit trees. They're so messy. You've got birds eating them, pooping everywhere, messing up cars, fruit falling on sidewalks. Edibles are just a nice idea." He said he wanted to bring me on to help the architectural design team "think big," "think outside the box," "wow 'em" in the design competition.

"You've got $1.67 per square foot to work with, Christie," the contractor states flatly, eyes cast down, scanning the spreadsheet in front of him. He's flown in from a nearby booming southwest town with his pressed white shirt, navy slacks, and practical loafers. He's very white with slicked-back strawberry blonde hair and a gold wedding band squeezing his ring finger. I imagine his life as pudgy.

❦

I LEAN BACK in my chair, arch my back, interlock my fingers behind my head, and drift off to my happy place, the seven-acre farm up north where Olivia was conceived, in spring of 2004 when the twenty-foot cherry trees blossomed and burst bushels, almost too many to dry, can, freeze, and bake into pies. I indulge in the memory of the farm whose land stretched to the Rio Grande, where the herds of elk grazed in December morning fog, ephemeral ghosts landing on lush alfalfa after having crossed Black Mesa near the Chama-Rio Grande confluence. I wasn't a hunter then. The elk migrated freely through the lower field, without my rifle scope sighted in on them.

On the farm, I allowed the plum thickets to cover the acequia bank, barely pruned the yearling heirloom fruit trees, let the orchard grass seed out. While clients in town demanded native penstemon be yanked from the root because "they're so ugly" when dormant, I relaxed into a less manicured rural life. The chickens roamed freely with access to the porch; poop plops on the concrete disgusted my mom. She'd scowl, "Why the hell don't you fence that part off, hon? Put those damn chickens in their own yard. They don't need to be comin' into yours!"

My evening walks down the fields through the bosque and onto the Rio Grande shore loosened the workday's rigidity. Client demands slipped from my professional, solve-it, spiff-it-up, make-it-pretty-now shoulders. "When will those plants start to grow?" and "Won't those be blooming soon? We leave for our other home at noon on Monday. I want to see something happen before we go." I'm supposed to know how to turn nature into a machine. I'm supposed to work her harder, whip her into shape, force her to grow faster so that I can earn more, be worth more, show how much I can do too.

But here along the river, I can meander with the current, laze in the cottonwood shade, hang chile ristras to dry from the portal on all sides of the house. I grind and package their hollow red shells and taste their spicy, earthen flavor throughout the year in posole, beans, carne adovada, and enchiladas.

These homegrown chiles aren't just for decoration.

❦

THE DEVELOPER CHIMES in about wanting trees, shade, color pop and something eye-catching. "We need to make this place different, attractive, up-and-coming." I wonder how to even get a shovel on the site for $1.67 per square foot.

"How about fake plants with a remote control?" I smirk.

"Yeah, you got it," the developer lights up as I adjust the wide leather belt around my waist, push my hair back, bite down on the pencil. With my waist thickening with age and my back getting stronger, some may say I'm pretty; I think I'm not bad looking but have to work hard at whatever pretty I have. I exercise. I watch what I eat. I shave my legs every day. I put makeup on each morning and tend to my hair most days. I'm not the kind of beautiful that wakes up flawless in the light of day, good to go with a quick toothbrushing and a pair of jeans. I see the lines on my face deepen over the years, brown age and sunspots become more prominent, a bit of droop to my neck and chin. You may say I'm the kind of beautiful of a vintage leather bag, not a Chanel with gold buckles and shiny patent straps.

The architect and the engineer hurry to the next subject: should the bathroom closets have doors? While they banter, fidget, and punch numbers on the calculator, I spin the mechanical chair round, shuttle myself up and down with the little lever at the seat, transporting myself beyond.

I feel the treasured corn kernels at my fingertips, garnet red like dried blood, burnished rust, indigo, and matte gold. I recall the October bumper corn harvest years ago in El Guique, when my nieces raced toward me, "Aunt Christie, Aunt Christie, look at this one!" peeling dried husks down swollen cobs. Better than any

Christmas present, the surprise hues of new treasures tugged from each regal stalk colored us alive.

I imagine each ear that formed, emerging as part of the male-female whole of the corn plant, embedded with eggs, the corn's female fertility map. The male tassels dazzle, showy, at the tip of the erect stalk, spouting granules of pollen that travel through seductive, microscopic silky ovule tunnels to fertilize the egg, eventually developing into upwards of one thousand juicy kernels.

Those kernels, suspended now as arced ristras tied together with jute twine in our kitchen twenty years later, hold tight to their cylindrical structures, witnessing cycles of seasons, rhythms of our daily lives. Each seed clings to the core in hushed dormancy, like the years tucked behind us yet visible now.

I locate myself in the air-conditioned conference room as we continue to examine the lines on paper, adjusting wall edges and width of sidewalks to squeeze a little more profitable square footage onto the lot. "If we cut that big 'ole cottonwood tree down, we can get at least two more units in," the contractor says.

"Yeah, and that neighbor to the east may sell us his lot," the developer adds. "Nothing there but a bunch of old junk cars. Bet he'd go for a nice check."

❦

I IMAGINE HOW much food could grow on this urban lot a stone's throw from the Rio Grande in the traditionally agricultural South Valley of Albuquerque. I imagine drawing lines on the paper that represent rows of annual crops—corn, beans, and squash, the Three Sisters rooted in generations of rich riparian soil. I see laden fruit trees and roadside neighborhood stands, like up north near El Guique, where farmers sell seasonal produce along the highway to tourists and locals hungry for homegrown flavor. What is a bushel basket of food worth compared to a two-story housing development? Does a patch of lettuce, tomatoes, herbs, and onions bring the neighbors and families together differently than the newly planned concrete patio? How can the old ways be worthy if the bottom line sees more profit in high-density housing?

The developer insists the complex should offer childcare, something for working parents that's convenient. "We could even have a playground centered in front of the apartments, near the laundromat, so moms can see their kids while folding clothes on the weekend. You know, a Tot Lot. Can you draw that up, Christie? Remember the playground-certified mulch that has to go in the fall zone around the play equipment. We don't want the kids getting hurt. And there will be a six-foot-tall fence so they can't get lost down along the river."

❧

WHILE I NOTE the added scope of service to my to-do list, I see in my mind's eye a photograph of me with Olivia from twelve years ago. In the image, I worked, shovel in hand, compost in wheelbarrow, tools and truck in the client's driveway. Olivia is about six months old with her sun bonnet and chubby legs poking out from the front pack harnessed to me. This was business as usual: another day at work with Mom.

The client pulled me aside that afternoon, asking me to put the shovel down, to come to the porch. I was sure he was angry about paying me for time billed to him while I was multi-tasking as a breastfeeding mom, doubling as mother and professional.

"Christie, I have to tell you something," he said. For once, his clenched jaws released. "I'm forty-seven years old and am still in therapy to this day, because my mom never had me with her, never spent time with me. I was raised by a nanny."

My daughter was born on January 7, winter in northern New Mexico and a time of frozen cash flow for me and any self-employed landscape design-build professional. Two weeks later, I bundled Olivia up in the front pack to take her to work pruning trees. Her little mouth puckered to my nipple as I lifted layers of wool while I selected branches to cut, buds to head off. In March, I breastfed her while supervising the guys as they constructed a stone wall and pulled over on the side of the road to change her diaper in the truck, careful to tuck the edges of the soiled wad back into its tape so turmeric-colored baby poop didn't ooze onto the floorboards or seats.

Nearly a year later she was with me again at one of my first big installation projects up north on a rural property recently purchased by a wealthy couple from back east. It's December, cold and the time of year when once again my bank account slows to a dormant crawl in sync with plant rhythms. Work screeched to a virtual halt. I went to check on the final touches of the installation and to get paid. This client, like some others, needed more nudging and reminding that his account was past due.

As he, his wife, and I stood there gazing out to the pasture and the newly installed landscape, admiring his accomplishments as a self-proclaimed country squire, I swayed my hips side to side, the ingrained motion of all moms with babies, trying to soothe an impatient Olivia, and reminded him of the payment owed. He and his wife looked out to the land as he pulled a check from his shirt pocket and dropped it on the ground in front of me.

"I hate to see a woman beg," he declared.

Bending down with Olivia hugged to my torso, I reached for the check, bit my lip, and thanked him for the payment. The squire, his wife, and I didn't make room for more words or pleasantries.

I buckled Olivia into her car seat, her blue saucer eyes open to mine, her trust and need softening the bitter brewing in me.

She still mends what had been broken.

❦

WE BEGIN TO wrap up the meeting, the engineer, architect, developer, contractor, and me. "Let's revise the plans with the new site layout and add a couple of units to the back corner. Christie, go ahead with the smaller apartment patios. Let's get that playground in there. And I want to see a lot of street-front parking and shops. We need to get people in there spending money," the developer cheers us on.

He pulls me aside in the parking lot. "You know, Christie, we'll get you a better design fee once we've earned the tax credits and can move beyond schematic design. For now, we have to do a kick-ass concept to win the design judges' interest. If we get them turned on to the project, they'll fund the next round of plans and implementation. Then we can pay you more."

The hourly fee I've agreed to covers about half the time required to complete the scope of work, but at least it's enough to pay the month's bills. While an architect's fees may range between 6 percent and 10 percent of the total building construction costs, a landscape architect's is typically a fraction of that, at about 6 percent of the landscape construction cost. So if the architect is getting about $20,000, the landscape architect earns about $2,000. Projects typically run over budget during the building phase, diminishing the budget for landscape even more. Clients ask for a "shrubbed up" parking lot good enough to satisfy city code, or the "best bang for their buck" on a residential landscape. Something maintenance-free and cheap.

I shake the developer's hand and head north toward home. The previous night's dream slips back in as I drive.

I'm sitting at the young landscape architect's desk. She's the one I went to graduate school with, the one who followed all the rules and progressed through the program at a safe, steady pace. I remember liking her well enough, but I couldn't tell what turned her on.

Now I'm in her office because she's done everything right and has been promoted from intern to a PLA in a reputable design-build firm.

Rather than position myself across from her in a chair, I choose to sit cross-legged on the floor. She rolls out the plans, reviews the design intent and scope of services and budget. The construction documents spell it all out in black and white, neat and tidy.

My eyes glaze over, I fidget on the floor and see scenes of manicured street medians with evenly spaced thornless, fruitless trees outside. Weed barrier and gravel replace leaves as groundcover. I let my eyes drift beyond the city toward the Jemez Mountain peaks to the west. Then, before I know it, I look down to see that I have taken a massive shit on the floor right in front of her as she drones on about the project.

I panic, lift up off my knees, and look around for toilet paper. But then realize I don't need it. That, in fact, I have left no mess.

When I turn to look at the pile, I see a heap of perfectly formed, shiny oblong elk turds.

❦

THE ALFALFA FIELDS of Algodones, north of Albuquerque, fill with acequia water, pooling in the low spots, spilling over at the ends of the planted rows. A tractor hums on the frontage road near the railroad tracks. The eighty-miles-per-hour interstate borders the green growth and old adobe neighborhoods.

I pull into Santo Domingo Pueblo to gas up, see the steep red rock incline of La Bajada ahead, the extreme topographic transition from the 5,300-feet elevation of Albuquerque to the 6,960-feet elevation of Santa Fe. I make it back to Santa Fe in time to pick Olivia up from school.

❦

WE DRIVE HOME chattering, sharing details about our day: my meeting in Albuquerque; her performance of a Spanish skit followed by cooking and serving a hot lunch to classmates. Sometimes on our way to and from school we listen to music, usually of Olivia's choosing. This is one of those days; we're both in a lively mood, chipper about getting home to chillax. Speaker turned up, music Bluetoothed in, I hear the raucous guitar and gritty vocals of AC/DC, one of our favorite bands.

My lips purse at the rhythmic chant of, "She takes you down easy, going down to her knees." I can't reach the volume dial quickly enough, and he hollers out another triumph, "Oh, she's blowing me crazy 'til my ammunition is dry!"

I wonder what of the lyrics Olivia hears. I wonder if she's simply grooving to the beat and letting go, listening to rad rock with Mom, or if she's taking in the words and meaning, if she hears who's on top.

"That one is so repetitive," I say, grabbing the device and skipping to the next song. "Let's listen to something else."

My hands tighten their grip on the steering wheel.

❦

THE SONG CONTINUES through my head, in counterpoint to the other words echoing in my head: "I hate to see a woman beg," "Fruit is so messy," "We'll pay you more later," "Cut the old cottonwood down," "Biggest bang for your buck."

Once at home with homework and a snack in front of Olivia, I find myself loading up my new Mauser .308, my very first rifle, my own, and fresh ammunition into the pickup. I strip off my skirt and blouse, pull on jeans and a long-sleeved cotton shirt, and lace up my hunting boots. I need to sight my rifle in for the upcoming elk hunt. I want to go shoot, to see clearly, focus and take aim at a practice target.

I drive the fifteen minutes from our home across the highway to the nearest public land at the Caja del Rio, a series of piñon-juniper-dotted mesas and sandy canyons that lead to the Rio Grande. Piles of empty shotgun shells and ammunition cartridges, TVs obliterated as close-range targets, broken glass, crunched Bud Light cans, and mini tequila, gin, and whiskey bottles reflect low fall sun. Old plywood, large plastic bottles, and discarded car hoods remain as makeshift bull's-eye targets. This national forest landscape lies broken by consumption, but it's the nearest place to take aim.

As I unload the shooting gear, I step over perfect piles of oval elk turds, some scattered into individual droplets, evidence of animals pooping in motion. Elk and deer cross here, following the drainages from neighboring gated golf course communities where fertilized grass and manicured ponds provide food and water. The elk hooves form pointy semicircles in scathed ground and press faded cans into stony soil.

I set up my target and shooting bench, put my cap and gloves on. With the rifle pressed firmly at ninety degrees from my shoulder—safety clicked off—I look through the scope. I see the red marker bull's-eye on butcher paper stapled to the plywood I brought from home as I breathe in, exhale, pull the trigger and say to myself, "This one's for you."

After shooting six groups—three shots each at six different mini targets—to make sure the rifle and scope are in line for a 150-yard shot, I pack up and fold the shooting bench into the pickup bed. The Mauser feels good. Right. We're getting to know each other.

On my way back home to Olivia, I allow scarred elk hooves, iridescent fascia skeins, slippery white bone, and leaky synovial fluid to throb in my palm. I fondle dank roots, cool water rivulets, and shells of seeds in the other as desired counterpoint truths. Price-per-square-foot delusions fade.

Olivia, the elk, and the seeds weave yesterday and tomorrow in the creased maps of my hands. Our territories aren't for the taking.

ELK DANCE

WE FINISH PACKING LAYERS of wool and camo, rain gear, extra socks, head lamps and batteries, ammunition, rope, come-alongs, tarps, game bags and the box of dry food. I'll pack the frozen green chile stew, squash soup, meat loaf, and sausage in the morning with the other cooler items.

I shower, taking extra time to wash my hair and shave my legs. I know it will be a few days until I enjoy the luxury of hot water. Al hops in as I step out and dry off. While he steams up the bathroom, I slather shea butter lotion over my thighs, belly, arms, neck, and calves. The excitement of the hunt in me, I strap my three-inch-wide cognac belt with round brass buckle around my chest, cinching it tightly across my nipples. My breasts bulge around the leather edges. Pantiless, I cat crawl onto the bed and wait for Al, sitting up with my knees crossed beneath my chin.

Shaking his wet hair on me with a big grin, he climbs onto the mattress, tugging my ankles toward him.

I push him over and climb on top, belted and ready. I taste my salt on his tongue after we've tugged each other over and under, finally landing over his face, my mouth hungry at his beard.

Tonight, pleasure. Tomorrow, the hunt.

❦

BEFORE DAYBREAK ON opening day, Al and I trek through thick

ponderosa pine forest at 8,500 feet in New Mexico's Unit 51 near Tres Piedras, just south of where Olivia and I had hunted spring turkeys. She's home with auntie Patty as I embark on another fall elk hunt. Walking with stealth, stopping, listening, scanning with binoculars, and sniffing the air for any indication of elk, Al and I read and respond to each other's bodies in the wordless dance of the hunt. The ebb and flow of instinct and information direct us. Fresh tracks, wet sign, heavy scent, our bodies follow the animals' leads and, when the animals don't reveal themselves, we study the maps. "Maybe if we hike that ridge we can look down into the canyon to see if they're grazing or across to the north-facing side where they may be bedded down."

I've never hunted big game alone before but want to be capable of the hunting, killing, skinning, butchering, and hauling on my own. Believing is one thing, doing is another. These animals are big; the country is big.

Al and I had set out together, as we have on multiple trips for elk, deer, oryx, and upland birds. He's had a gun in his hand since the time he learned to walk. Surrounded and raised by people who hunt, Al hunts multiple days per week, five months of the year. Time on the prairie, in the mountains, and through sage scrub hills in his fifty-five years continue to form the animal in him. Our years together have been an extension of his migratory patterns from north to south and back again, New Mexico to North Dakota—the grasslands, foothills, and mountains in between the hunting ground for us both. We live professional and domestic lives together as schedules allow, his time wrapped around and prioritizing hunting season. Grouse and partridge in early fall, pheasant in late fall and early winter, quail in early winter, and big game antelope, deer, and elk when a tag becomes available.

Our extended families merged with ease. His six siblings and their kids folded Olivia into the extensive cousin clan and countless aunts and uncles welcomed me too. They and the local North

Dakotans all said, "We never have seen Al bring anybody home. You're the first."

He was my first beau to meet my family since my last break up ten years earlier. Pappa handed Al the pliers to fix the back porch door, they putzed through handyman chores with ease.

We were at home together.

❦

THIS DAY, AS we move together under dawn's new light, Al bites, "Christie, I want you to stop when I stop. I don't stop for no reason."

"I didn't know you had stopped," I respond, a flush of shame and embarrassment rise through my belly. He marches past me, steely eyed, militaristic, in a different direction. "Where are you going?" I ask.

"That way. I'm going to do what I do," he states flatly, disgusted.

"OK, would you like to let me know where you're going or if I'm included?"

"I would like you to follow me and do what I do for another thirty minutes, and then we'll go back to the pickup," he snaps.

"OK." The levity of hope, looking toward new tracks and possible spot-and-stalk opportunities sink to lead in my feet.

❦

MEMORIES OF PREVIOUS hunts churn through me, the moments we moved through with ease, in equal exchange. "You know, sometimes we get one during the middle of the afternoon, when they're not even supposed to be on their feet." We had reminisced about the Vermejo cow elk, the thirteen-year-old one whose spine I broke with one shot. Not the correct or best shot but lethal nonetheless.

The Springer elk, too, with a handful of others, grazed the slope at two in the afternoon. And an elk stood with her eyes on us as Al drove up the narrow canyon just past Amos tank where we had lunched and rested, a few ridges southeast of Hopewell Lake in New Mexico Game Management Unit 51. That was my sixth elk hunt, the one where I almost did it by myself.

Looking over my right shoulder, I had blurted, "Look at that one right there, just standing there staring at us!"

"What?" asked Al.

"A cow elk. Keep going, slow, slow, slow. Don't stop. Don't spook her," I instructed. We drove two hundred yards farther, pulled the pickup over and got out. I hurried with the rifle, my pack and camo jacket. Al sat in the driver's seat. "Come on, let's go!" I whispered with urgency, "Get the sticks!"

"Do you want me to come with you?" he asked tentatively.

"Of course, come on!"

"Sometimes I wonder if you want me in the field with you."

I didn't know how to tell the truth, how to put myself first, and I didn't have the confidence to back it up.

It was true, I had been wanting to hunt big animals on my own, wondered if I could do it. Could I do the tracking, the spotting through binoculars, patiently waiting for movement and an opportunity to make a stalk? Could I get the rifle set up, judge the shooting distance correctly, and remain steady to make a lethal shot? Could I follow through with splitting the animal open, butchering her into packable parts, and hauling her to the pickup?

Am I strong enough yet? Experienced enough? Do I have enough kill drive in me?

But this time, I still believe I need Al with me. Maybe we can function as a team in this setting. Maybe if I need him, he will want to stay.

❦

WE PRESS ON, steely resolve thickening between us. No tracks, no sign, no elk or other wildlife except ravens taunting atop spruce and flitting songbirds fussing over each other. We lunch in silence, the tailgate's hard metal beneath us, baby carrots, hummus, kale leaves, lunchmeat, and whole wheat bread passed back and forth. Flavorless.

❧

AS WE HEAD toward a new canyon for the afternoon and evening walk, I step over a fresh track and wet soil in the middle of the two-track road. A cow elk had just crossed, stopped and peed while we ate, not more than two hundred yards from us, but out of view behind a knoll. I muffle the instant flutter inside, knowing my yes magnifies his no.

The hush of sunset closes the day's conversation on all fronts. Today's hunting is over. The enclosure of the Airstream, supper, and bed loom.

Driving back through darkness, glassy red deer eyes dart across the highway, just missing the truck grill. I pull over to call Olivia and Patty. Maybe home will warm me up.

"Hi, Mom!" Olivia chirps. Tears flow to the lilt of her voice. I feel her body held close to my chest, smell her lavender-scented shampoo, her supple cheek on mine through the phone line. "Why are you crying, Mom?" she asks, "What's wrong?"

"I just miss you, hon. How was your day? What's for supper? What's Edmund up to?"

"We're having chicken, broccoli, and rice. Edmund is out on the prowl. Haven't seen him since just after school."

"Could you do something for me, Olivia? I need a big favor."

"Of course, Mom. What is it?"

"Could you do a dance for me? An elk dance? Tonight? I need your magical juju. The hunt isn't looking too good so far."

As her ballet instructor says with a confident knowing, "That girl was meant to dance. She is going to be a dancer. She will be great!"

I imagine her choreographing and dancing the elk. How will she move her feet? Her arms and hands? Will her fingertips skim the ceiling or drape to the floor? Will she smile or reserve expression for her feet and legs? I imagine the elk coming through Olivia, graceful beasts, solid and sure yet light-footed, agile, there in Santa Fe in the comfort of home, while I move my body up canyons, through oak, and over ridges. She dances it. I work it.

The pause on her end magnifies my desperation. Maybe I've asked too much. Gone too far.

"Mom. I will. I'll dance. I'll do it tonight."

❦

BACK AT CAMP after driving in silence, I begin the separation, "I would like to hunt alone tomorrow." "OK," Al replies, flat. We tiptoe around each other, avoid the truth in between. We've fashioned a long-distance relationship for nine years now, migrating seasonally back and forth between North Dakota and New Mexico. Both of us middle-aged and single most of our lives, we know better than to force a conventional arrangement. Even after marrying the year before, we don't live together most of the time. We regularly migrate 2,458 miles across the Great Plains—our destination each other—orienting seasonally to the harvest and hunt for food. We live separately and come together by hot instinct, contrary to domestic convention and routine. Ours is the first marriage for us both, at forty-five and fifty-four. Our two weddings in two states celebrated a love like no other. We vowed not to make vows, knowing a future could not be promised.

Our wedding menu reflected our garden, our hunts. We gathered it all by hand to serve over-the-top love: shots of chilled sweet pea and mint soup with truffle oil; pan-seared oryx with cured tomato and arugula; piquillo peppers stuffed with pheasant; marinated and grilled elk loin and vegetable skewers; stuffed squash with fennel, onion, and parmesan; cured and smoked pike with chile and lime on crostini. I sifted cocoa and whipped cream into a triple decker cake, decorating it with hundreds of grouse, partridge, and quail feathers, situating each miniature quill just so.

Guests stayed late to have seconds—and lick their fingers.

Tonight, I know his teaching and my learning have plateaued. I am defining my own way, making my own tracks. We hunt for different reasons.

It's late. The dishes rest on the towel. The candle is blown out. The alarm is set. We go to bed, without touch or talk. We toss. Turn.

Four thirty the next morning, I get up, slip on a cotton bra, panties, wool long johns, fleece, and camo. My boots, stiff with yesterday's mud, compress sore feet into laced confines. I load the magazine, place it along the console on the passenger side in the pickup near the .308 along with lunch, water, maps, and binoculars. I lug the backpack—enough in it for one—onto the passenger seat.

Back inside the Airstream, I tiptoe to turn the lights and propane off. Al musters a "Good luck."

I melt, dribbling, "I would rather hear 'I love you. I will be there for you.'"

He lies there, his sigh as heavy as the doughy foam mattress beneath him.

"This is the part when you get up to give your wife a hug," I appeal.

He pulls himself to his feet, goes through the motion of holding me.

I stiffen. "I'm not as good a hunter as you. I don't know what went wrong."

"Come get me if you need me." He lets go.

❦

AT CUNNINGHAM CANYON twenty minutes later, I park, turn the windshield wipers and lights off, hop down from the pickup, wipe my eyes, and tell myself, "Now go do what you want. Go hunt."

I click the magazine into place, then push one cartridge into the chamber, safety on. Up the logging road, misty canyon below, moisture hangs on pine needles, muffles my steps. Low clouds obscure the ridge ahead. I know this canyon, but the rain camouflages it. We are new to each other—me alone; it wet. I breathe harder while gaining elevation. Putting one foot in front of the other, I relax into the ponderosa-aspen ridge. The scope and rifle over my shoulder point to the sky. Clusters of oaks open to a grassy overlook where two boulders punctuate craggy bark. They support my back and smudge my outline as I squat, looking through the binos. I see blonde rumps, blurry in the drizzle, and yank my eyes back from scanning the clearing.

Two elk graze below.

They're relaxed at the base of the opposite slope, muzzles to ground, no indication of alarm. My hands shake as I pull the rifle to my shoulder. Heavy sleet-snow obscures my vision and, as I position the scope to my eyes, I realize the precipitation has wetted and fogged the glass. I forgot to put the lens cap on last night and to check it this morning. There was no precipitation since we began, so a wet, foggy lens hadn't crossed my mind. The range finder, too, is wet as I try to determine the distance between me and the elk. I know they're close enough, but without visible antlers I can't tell their sex. I sit and watch, crouched down, butt in wet duff. "Calm the fuck down." I grind my teeth, jaws clenched. Hands shaking, I lift the binos to look again. I see clearly that one elk is a bull, and maybe the other is a spike, a young bull with two single, straight antler points—or a cow? I can't tell. I decide to move farther down the hill, wiping scope, bino, and range finder lenses with my shirt sleeve.

Other elk crackle fallen timber with their heavy hooves on the slope to the south. The elk move up into the dense brush. I'm still unsure of their sexes: is there a cow? One grazes, his head obscured behind dense coniferous cover but revealing enough antler tip that I know I can't position the crosshairs on him. I move closer, sit, remove my pack, get ready. They're at about one hundred yards, well within range. They meander slowly until finally she turns her head. No antlers. The bull stays just behind her. I inch closer and get set up, my knees bent, bottom on the ground, heels dug in, facing downhill. I can practically hear them chewing.

"Steady the rifle on your knees, Christie Green," I tell myself. Steady. Steady. Scope is still wet, foggy. Her blonde butt faces me squarely. Not a broadside shot. No shot for me, inexperienced in shooting from varied orientations or at animals whose positions are anything but bull's-eye perfect. This is not part of the two-hundred-yard, solid rest, broadside formula. "What the fuck do I do next?" Breathe. Look closer. The bull moves from behind her. Now I don't have to worry about the bullet penetrating her mass and going into his. I see her front left leg, lift the rifle, cross hairs of the scope slightly below the top of the leg. If I'm at thirty to thirty-five yards, shouldn't I aim lower because the bullet will fly high? "Take the shot, Christie, take the fucking shot."

I pull the trigger, watching the elk through the scope to see if she's injured, if she'll run, if I'll find her, or if I'll be able to track, fire another shot to kill, cut, butcher and pack. Will I be able to do what's required?

The rifle's sharp clap echoes up the canyon. The other elk are long gone. Nothing. These two do nothing. They don't even flinch. She looks over her back directly at me, her mouth chomping the grass she had just tugged from the ground.

I missed.

I load another bullet in the chamber, she turns, her ass faces me. And then they bolt, uphill to the north. They're finally on to me.

My backpack buckled across my hips, rifle and binos at my neck again, I follow their sign and tracks up this mini elk highway, a route they've pounded many times before. I continue, knowing they're long gone, but I see the two elk again directly to my right; I caught up with them, but they jet up craggy granite through the oaks to cover.

That's the last I saw of them or any other elk.

What would Al have done? What would he have said? How would he have coached me?

Olivia comes to mind as I surrender, head back. I imagine her elk dance. Her voice saying, "Hi, Mom. I miss you, Mom." We dance through the woods at her tempo, her leisure, her aimless direction, propelled by curiosity, and creativity, not by the desire to conquer. She comes to me, nudges my squishy boots, lifts me to the pickup where heat and food console.

I slog through the rest of the day, feigning ability, wanting another lucky chance. My gut sinks as I start the engine, shift into gear, head back to camp.

❧

PERIPHERAL VISION, OR indirect vision, occurs outside the point of fixation, away from the center of gaze. Most of the area in the visual field is included in peripheral view. There are far areas at the edges of the visual field; areas nearly adjacent to the center of the gaze; and the midperipheral zone, somewhere between in focus and just out of range. Practically at my fingertips, yet out of reach, the elk slip away. Did I see clearly?

When attempting to discern stars and constellations in the night sky, peripheral vision is often more effective than looking directly at the star. Softening the gaze and moving it slightly away from the desired object may increase the eyes' ability to distinguish the star.

The loss of peripheral vision while retaining central vision is known as tunnel vision.

Locked eye to eye what did the elk see in me? Did I appear as predator, intruder, or animal? Would such an intimate gaze allow or dissolve my aim during future electric encounters?

❧

AL IS THERE in bed when I arrive back at the Airstream. He's been in bed all day. I imagined that he would be out enjoying his freedom. He sits up, surprised to find it already dark. We talk, touch, tiptoe closer to each other over pheasant green chile stew and a glass of wine, the heater humming in the background, steam on the windows.

"Ah damn, the scope!" He rests his forehead in his palm. "Should have put the cap on, I knew that."

"I saw them right away, Al. I couldn't believe they were there. In the mist and fog, their butts looked like a mirage, like they were moving in slow motion. I got so close. Closer and closer and they never smelled or saw me . . . But I missed."

"You did everything right. Just right. It happens sometimes. I've missed too. Everyone has. Let's head back to Cunningham tomorrow. I bet they'll be there in the morning." Al comforts.

Fewer words are exchanged the later it gets. He pulls my layers off, slides socks over my feet, rubs my heels and toes. I stand over him in the Airstream's baby blue shower, nozzle spraying suds off my shoulders, down my inner thighs, onto my calves, a bubbly white river down the drain. Tightness in my body loosens with the wet heat. Al watches me from the bed nest. His legs stretch long, chest hairs cast curly shadows. Some of what we rely on to mend, to move forward, some of what's best between us, goes unspoken. My head at his feet, his tongue slips between each clean toe on both feet as I slather lotion everywhere else. The pop of his lips sucking my big toe evokes our first laugh in two days.

Throughout the last day, we hunt together, returning to our dance of strategy and stealth, whispering, listening, looking. Sharing a chatty lunch from the tailgate, spotting fresh tracks in the skiff of snow, smelling musky elk scent from fresh droppings and pee. "I wonder if I should have stood up or tried to lay down? But they were slightly uphill, what would the bullet have done?" I obsess over every detail from the day before, trying to get it right, at least in my mind. I want to know how to be the hunter that doesn't falter.

"The bullet would have been dead-on. You should have fired right at the kill zone. Only if you were farther than two hundred yards would you have needed to make adjustments. You shouldn't have doubted yourself."

We've been on the heels of a small herd all day, so close that steam rises from yellow pee near a stump at our feet. But we never get a glimpse. "Let's head back to that saddle we set up on the first day . . . you know, where all the sign was," Al suggests.

We head from Cunningham to another drainage farther west, hiking a couple of hours to a ridge with lush aspens on either side. The saddle opens, allowing visibility to both sides from a meadow. We sit. Glass. Shift position occasionally, walk a little more, and wait.

Night falls, the legal shooting time ends. The hunt is over.

"Let's walk out this way, along the open, less brushy slope."

Two hours later, under dim light of a waxing moon and no clear sense of where the pickup is parked, we realize we're lost. "Well, I know if we keep walking north, we'll run into the highway and can hitch a ride. That's damn far, though," Al laments.

"I'm pretty sure we're just at the top of Maquinitas Canyon. I think we'll intersect the road to the west where we're parked if we keep walking." The packs are heavier now on day five, at nightfall, and with lunch long since digested. Our headlamps shine down to the topo map, and Al's compass confirms we're heading north.

"This is right. Let's keep going. It just feels farther, longer." I encourage us, hoping this isn't a real lost where all that is known and recorded on the map appears unintelligible, irrelevant in this seemingly foreign place. How did we get here, and which way do we go now? Roads, fence lines, stock tanks—human markers of place—elude us. This time, we trek the terrain, hoping our instinct finds the way.

Then, out of the corner of my eye, I see the bend of the side road, the red of the pickup taillight reflecting our headlamp light.

❦

WE PACK UP the Airstream, hitch it up and head south. Elk criss-cross the road in front of us, eyes shining red in the headlights. They're safe now, revealing themselves to us as dark shadows moving from meadow to saddle to ridge under the cover of night. Barbed wire boundaries, asphalt, and land ownership can't confine them.

I imagine the elk flesh under my fingernails while cutting through the muscle, tendon, hide, bone. I imagine the strips of freezer tape stuck to the counter, the Sharpie markers, the waxy butcher paper, the hum of the grinder, Al's singing, and our joyful ease while cutting meat all week.

But with no elk to hoist from the pickup, the house sits empty.

"Come here," I command. Al slips into bed, freshly showered. His weight rocks on top of me, pins me to the sheets, hard, fast. My lips feel the wet of his beard, mint of his toothpaste tongue. My arms overhead, his palms hold my forearms down, my legs grab his waist. We fuel each other's forgetting.

My breasts roll to my side as I turn over, drifting off. Our finger-tips touch beneath the blankets. A faint "Good night, darling," tickles my neck as Al snuggles into sleep against me.

Olivia surfaces in a dreamlike haze; I can almost see her. She danced the elk to me that morning in the sleet. They came to me through her tippy toes, her lengthened arm and flexed legs. Olivia, my most right choice.

The cow elk appears through the mist. I see her rump. Her ears alert. Her mouth chomping the fescue. Her hooves pressing into the dank soil. I smell her. I believe she's still young; the youth in her body like a little girl as she makes her escape.

Where will we cross paths next?

FULL

Moon and sun are aligned.

She is fully exposed, illuminated, visible from the earth.

DREAM STAGES

Dreams occur during Rapid Eye Movement (REM) sleep.

Intense brain activity, absence of motor function except eye muscles and diaphragm.

Increased blood flow to brain, penis, and clitoris.

Believed to be a minority of overall sleep experience.

2017–2020

FIVE DEER

"IT'S NOT A MATTER of if you'll get some deer, darlin," my cousin Amanda chirps over the phone. "But how many you'll get. They're all over down here; they're like rats!" A sales representative for dairy cattle nutrient supplements, Amanda is thirteen years younger than me and lives with her husband, Justin, a veterinary chiropractor, and their two young sons.

I didn't kill a cow elk during the hunt last month at Cunningham Canyon, so I've decided to come here two weeks before Christmas, to Justin's family's land in central Texas, to hunt. I want to fill the freezer to feed myself and my daughter, Olivia, over the coming year, and the bag limit of four deer seems to justify the twenty-hour round trip. The opportunity to stay and visit with Amanda and her family makes the journey that much more of a treat. I love my Texan relatives, all twang and iced tea, rhinestone, giddy-up, cowboy-boot love. We tiptoe around politics at the dinner table and opt for, "How did the boys do in baseball this year? How was Brent's cotton harvest? Have you seen Joe's new house?" Conversation safely cached in care for each other's daily lives.

Gearing up for the trip, I pack for my first deer hunt without Al. He's opted to hunt with a friend in Kansas after the holidays rather than join me with my family. The passenger seat is empty, the cooler holds fewer snacks than usual, and there's only a single thermos mug in the cup holder. It will be a quiet ride.

Kissing Olivia and Al goodbye, I buckle up and head out,

descending through canyons and piñon-juniper scrub from Santa Fe toward the Plains. The Sangre de Cristo Mountains shrink in my rearview mirror, my field of vision expands, and curves diminish as I enter straight-line worlds of wide, flat, backcountry highways and fence-lined ranches. Driving through southeastern New Mexico and the Texas Panhandle, I witness what had historically been grassland—the southernmost expanse of the Great Plains—transition to soil scoured by cattle hooves and mouths. Once expertly and intuitively managed between indigenous people and bison, with grass high enough to graze a horse's belly, the land is barely a dusty two-inch stubble in this economy of "get it while you can." Graze it, plough it, pump it, and push the byproduct waste right back into it through manure, methane, frack water, and agricultural chemical runoff.

Deeply rooted perennial grasses once held the soil, percolated water, sequestered carbon, and provided wildlife habitat and forage. Bison adapted to weather extremes and migratory grazing without the constraint of fences. Both plant and animal stewards have become relics since the turn of the century. Belief in the power of the plough to transform so-called useless, unproductive land into food and profit catalyzed the transformation.

Settlers followed the Old Santa Fe Trail and arrived here from the East Coast in 1909 with hope as wide as the horizon. Congress encouraged settlement of the Great Plains through the Homestead Act, which doubled the amount of land settlers could own to 320 acres, half a section.

The gritty determination of twentieth-century homesteaders clinging to one more ploughed furrow, another season's seed sown, and "Maybe this year we'll get a bumper crop" surfaces in my mind. Images by Depression-era photographer Dorothea Lange, along with my grandfather's tales of hobos walking the railroad tracks looking for a living and food, drift through me. "We didn't have much," he recounted, "but my mom always found a little something to share. Everyone was welcome."

While working on my landscape architecture thesis about the cultural and ecological effects of fracking in western North Dakota, I met with Lynn Helms, then the head of the North Dakota Oil and Gas Division, to try to understand the politics and decision-making behind the state's aggressive pumping policy. "Well, do you think you may want to hold off on pumping all of the Bakken Formation?" I asked.

That question eats at me now as I drive through the southern end of the fracked Plains. Tumbleweeds are stacked high against barbed wire fence lines held taut by weathered wood posts. No signs of grassland or bison. No remnants of a system once alive with soil, calculated animal husbandry, and stewardship.

The land is whipped.

"What do you mean?" he replied, looking puzzled.

"Well, if we maintain that we still don't know enough about the effects of fracking on water supplies, on the geology below ground and on the fossil fuel reserves, maybe we should take it slow or only test drill less sensitive areas."

His frenzied, eager eyes gazed beyond the sterile conference table. His assistant looked at her wristwatch again. "Nope," he said, flashing a confident grin. "We know we have a good thirty to forty years' supply of oil and gas. We're going for it."

Going for it. I had my own experience of going for it when I profited from eighty-four-hour work weeks with double overtime pay, meal tickets, and subsidized lodging during the *Exxon Valdez* oil spill. The oil corporations lavished exorbitant resources to demonstrate a commitment to cleaning up and "doing right." I enjoyed catered gourmet breakfasts and lunches, double lobster tail dinners and a generous per diem on top of the pay that funded a year of my undergraduate education.

It was good while it lasted.

Now, for mile after mile, the pumpjacks lob their rhythmic steel helmets up and down, plunging into the earth, penetrating miles of strata, pulling up fossil fuels through hydraulic-fractured veins. The same companies running the pumpjacks also flog the land into surrendering genetically modified cotton, corn, wheat, and sorghum. Upwards of three million acres of cotton have been cultivated in the southern Plains alone, rotated with dryland wheat. Productivity is coaxed with heavy doses of ammonium-rich chemicals. Neither cotton nor corn is suited for this arid landscape. Both require more water than is available as this portion of the Ogallala Aquifer, which flows under eight Great Plains states, is at risk of imminent depletion. US Geological Survey aquifer studies confirm that we're pumping water out eight times faster than it's being replenished.

I pass through Muleshoe, Texas, on Highway 214, just south of Mamma's and Pappa's land, now owned and managed by my uncle Chris, Mom's younger brother. The blinking light, grain elevator, and gas station remind me of childhood trips to my paternal grandparents' house. The sulfur smell of pumpjack oil through the car vents indicated our arrival in Denver City, near the current fracking hubs of Odessa and Midland. The aroma meant home to me then and a fragmentation of home now. The land was divided, extracted, pumped, and ploughed even that many years ago. I just hadn't seen, hadn't understood.

I cling to what was, a snow-globe memory of rural America: casseroles shared in wheat-field harvest gatherings with Mamma and my aunt Marty. We lapped up homemade Fourth of July peach ice cream and ballfield fireworks. My brother, cousins, and I would race to the irrigation ditch, scooping up as many galvanized siphon tubes as our adolescent arms could carry, placing one end in the ditch, over the soil mound, and the other end into the furrow. We alternated a cupped palm with sucking lips in the circular end of the pipe, creating suction enough to coax Ogallala water from the ditch to the furrows. Who would be the one to pump the most tubes the fastest to quench the rows' thirst? Shucking corn on the back porch, snapping green beans, and grilling homegrown beef that we harvested, prepped, cooked, and ate together, a way of life sown in eager, young hands.

We made a living, a life. Family was, and is, home.

Another cousin, Brent, is a cotton farmer in the Panhandle. We see each other a couple of times a year when I make my way back to the family land for a holiday—all of the cousins, aunts and uncles gathered around the kitchen island, scooping tortilla chips in melted Velveeta and Pace Picante salsa dip. "How have y'all been?" "How's business?" and "How's Olivia doing in dance?" were passed around as freely as the Sweet'n Low for oversized-glasses of cold-brewed Lipton Iced Tea.

I recently asked him about the Water for Sale signs, punctuation points along the flat highway expanse. "That's water the farmers are selling to the oil and gas companies. They need it for fracking; the farmers sell it as a commodity." Water that's already facing extinction is being sold from one extractive industry to the other— one hoping to last longer than the other before the resource goes belly-up.

"What will you do in four years?" I ask my cousin, who's ten years younger than me and a father of three. Brent's wide blue eyes with doll-like lashes search the floor at his Anderson Bean-booted feet. His dinner plate sits cold—gravy drying, gristle scraps pushed aside, the fork at rest. "I don't know. I don't have time to think about that or plan. I am just doing all I can to make a living the way I know how. I don't have time or resources to find another way, another crop to farm or way of life. I suppose we'll just have to pick up and leave when the water's gone and then I don't know what."

It's a ten-hour drive through the Plains. Some say, "It's a whole lotta nothin' out there!" I feel that whole lotta nothin' in my rear end and shift position in the driver's seat. I reach for easy finger food like almonds, apples, and elk jerky to pull from the little cooler. Sage scrub, cholla, opuntia, and intermittent winterfat rise, flaccid green and puffy white against dusty, red soil. A roadrunner flits across the frontage road to the south. Turkey vultures glide, drunkenly teetering in the hazy distance. I imagine the deer I'll shoot, their skeletons pulled apart by coyotes then picked clean by vultures and other raptors and rodents.

Windmills and homesteads, gas tanks, combines, tractors, and disc ploughs parked for winter remind me of the neighbor names attached to each place: Brorman, Gruhlkey, Skaggs, Myers. Their families extend into ours—the wheat, the cattle, the church pews. Our common familial ties connect shared hardship and bounty.

I make the transition to the rolling oak woodland hills of central Texas and arrive at my cousin's just in time for supper. Amanda's hug and pearly smile welcome me. Her boys, Hudson and Hayes, herd at my feet, hot grease vibrates in the iron skillet, and roasting dinner rolls waft to my nostrils. Homegrown chicken fried steak is on the menu, complete with mashed potatoes and gravy—what I recognize as homey comfort.

We sit down to eat, and I ask Justin about how to get set up for tomorrow's hunt and about the habits of the deer—when they come in to graze or lay down to rest. He sort of chuckles, telling me, "This isn't like the hunts you do in New Mexico, Christie. We have feeders that are programmed to go off first thing in the morning. They sling corn out for the deer to eat. The blinds are set up within a few yards of the feeders. It's really just a matter of showing up."

I can't imagine a hunt where I just show up. Some of my hunts that have lasted up to seven days, like the bow hunt four years earlier, have been unsuccessful, one shift of the wind blowing my chances at the kill. Gregory Cajete, a native of Santa Clara Pueblo just south of El Guique, shares the essence of the hunter of good heart. "The hunter of good heart was a bringer of life to his people: he had to have not only a very intimate knowledge of the animals he hunted but also a deep and abiding respect. While he tracked the animal physically, he also tracked the animal ritually, thereby understanding at a deeper level his relationship with the animal he hunted."

plexiglass windows that flip open with ease—I set up in the folding chair that's been left on the floor and open three windows to see out to the corn feeder forty yards away. The hum of wind turbines echoes through quiet hills, the only audible sound besides cardinals emerging to sing the new dawn awake. I wait, sitting still, listening, looking.

The monotone metal bin chugs to life, spinning round and round, casting GMO corn kernels in a circular path on the open ground. About fifteen deer congregate, their delicate lips plucking the rich grains one by one from soil to mouth. Positioning the .308 Mauser snug to cheek and shoulder, I take aim, the crosshairs of the scope situated on the one doe standing broadside. The morning light is barely bright enough for me to see the kill zone just above and behind her front leg. I breathe in, exhale out, place my index finger on the steel trigger and pull. The other deer flee. This one falls, feet flailing upward, white tail a descending blur.

I steady the scope. Is she dead? Do I need to take another shot? Her body spasms with a flutter of hooves and then a final stillness. I wait for the deer to return; they often will after a scare.

She lies on the dusty ground as rising sunlight casts new shadows. Her tail, once the bright-white bounce of "follow me this way," is now deflated, motionless. I wait, my chest less turbulent with each passing minute.

They return, just as many deer as before, teetering on dainty hooves. Cagey. I scope a few does farther out, away from the feeder. Looking through sage scrub and oak cover, I search for a hint of real hunting circumstance, where scanning with binos, sitting still, and patience are a must. I pull the rifle up to my shoulder, snug to my right cheek, and settle the crosshairs on a doe at about one hundred yards.

A single shot takes the graze from her mouth, the air from her lungs, the ground from her feet.

The next day is much the same. I arrive in the early dawn, shoot one deer, wait for the others to return, and shoot another. I kill four in all, three does and a buck.

Back at Amanda's house, I skin and butcher the deer under the carport, separating hind and front quarters from the backbone, severing the heads from the necks, cutting away tender meat one muscle group at a time. I rub the wet, dark clay between their hooves, see the pulverized corn between ungulate teeth, feel the stubborn ticks clinging to the thin skin around their anuses and genitals, touch the long, delicate lashes over dead, glazed eyes. The questions I hold about the ethics of an easy kill circulate again through my brain as rhythmically as the knife in my hand separates hide from muscle. Am I worthy of this meat? Is their sacrifice for my sustenance justified?

Circling on their tricycles, my cousin's little boys ask their mama, "Why are Christie's hands all bloody? What's she doing?" The mutts at my feet await a meaty scrap.

Justin also watches me, asking if I need help as I use the tailgate as a makeshift butcher station. "I have no idea how to do what you're doing," he observes. "We usually just take them over to the processor and have him pull the backstraps and make sausage out of the rest." His gentle curiosity and generous provision of home, land, and family soften the edge of the shoulds pressing hard against me. Should I have kept and made use of all of the organs— not just the meat, hides, and skulls? Should I make it easier and eat locally grown beef instead? Should I have travelled this far? Should I be taking time away from my daughter? Should I hand over the butchering to someone else?

On the final morning I swallow my tea, read a quick story to Hudson on the couch, and savor breakfast burritos with Texas salsa in the kitchen around the coffee pot with Amanda and Justin. Then I pack up my things, carefully arranging the hind and front quarters, heads, backstraps and tenderloins of the four deer in the back of the Prius. "We just made wonderful memories!" Amanda hollers with a bigger-than-Dallas grin as I pull away. Knowing the drive home will be hot in the car, I stop at the local Kum & Go convenience store to load up on ice. This winter month feels more like early spring, and I'm concerned the meat might spoil.

I begin the journey home to Santa Fe, depletion staring back at me with each flat mile. The land is hard. I pass rectangular bales of cotton wrapped in neon pink, yellow, and blue plastic and labelled with code numbers and letters for processing and export. Woody cotton stems and bolls stand stripped, raw.

I press on, thankful for the drone of miles under the tires. This meat will provide for many holiday dinners, neighborhood potlucks, and weeknight casseroles. As I drive through section after section of flat, muted Panhandle land, simple elements of seed, soil, and water stare back at me as large-scale, industrialized versions of themselves.

The migratory sandhill cranes, Canada geese, mallards, and snow geese search for a wet place to land in the frack-sludge ponds. The whitetails and pronghorns learn barbed wire and asphalt navigation, their hooves clacking across paved surfaces as headlights blur by.

I lose count of mileage and silos, Water For Sale signs and proud 4-H posters. I roll on from winding county roads to state two-lane highways to the interstate, avoiding semitruck traffic.

I arrive home past midnight to a dull porch light and the living room silent except for Edmund's faint meow as he whisks through my ankles out the sliding glass door. Al and Olivia are asleep.

Rather than heading to bed, I return to the car and lift the hatchback, releasing the scent of the deer. I reach into the back where multiple hooves protrude through coolers and tarps of ice, and feel a leg, a head, a hide, pulling one out at a time. I lift them to my nose, inhale.

There is dried blood caked in my fingernails. My body feels the drum of the road, the shots fired, the knives sharpened, the butchering cuts made. I want to take the animals into the house. I want to place them on my bed, to position them around Al and me as we unbutton each other's clothes, trace tongues over curves, move with hushed urgency. I want to commune with their bodies and his body to undo all the pumped, ploughed, fracked, and triggered demands.

But I return to the deer. I lift the three doe heads, one by one, into my open palms, walking them to a wooden shelf-like altar that's secured about five feet high on the picket fence in the east yard. I position them with the smallest—the second doe I shot—toward the front in the center. Her dainty lashes lie flat, her matte black nose puckers dry, ears shrink toward her severed neck. The other two does flank the young one, as if still able to protect her from both sides.

Once inside the house, I run a stockpot full of water and lower the buck's head with antlers into the pot. His bulging eyes glare back, stray fat dangling from the skull in the sloshing water. I turn the burner to low, so the head can simmer through the night, the water cooks flesh from bone.

I see the altar centered in the frame of the kitchen window. I will look from here in two days to watch Al driving up our dirt road toward his Kansas hunt as the distance between us grows.

Over the coming months I will witness the hides on the heads desiccate and flake off, the eyes sink into withered orbs, the skulls reveal themselves—cranial cracks splitting like tiny creeks coursing through a still, white topography. A succession of insects, from flies to maggots to shiny beetles, will perform their tasks of eating the flesh, breaking death down farther.

The wrens, ravens, thrashers, finches, and sparrows will congregate to pluck the writhing vermin with their curved beaks. Their poop, sloppy spills of moss green and white, will dot the fence and fertilize the soil below. The stench of decomposition will intensify during the warmer months, wafting through the window as I cook, offending neighbors as they walk their leashed dogs to the dry riverbed.

I wonder what Hudson and Hayes will remember of me cutting

deer on the tailgate. What will Olivia think of my bloody hands at the kitchen counter, wrapping meat into neatly labelled white packages? What dinner-table stories will Brent and Amanda's kids overhear? Will they learn the feel of the siphon tube, S wrench, cattle prod?

Who will taste the deer and care where they came from? Where will the fawn plant her pointy hooves, press herself into the earth, and take flight, skyward, boundless?

GILA JAKE

"I WOULD LIKE TO go to the Gila to hunt alone. I want to hunt turkeys solo, to get one on my own," I tell my brother, who's been my new hunting partner lately.

Al is in North Dakota. We finally unraveled completely, let each other go after his Kansas deer hunt and seven months apart. His, "I want to do what I want to do. I don't want to change. I don't want to try anymore," still weighs heavy inside. We haven't spoken since filing for divorce, since his last trip down to clean out his stuff, pack up, and return north one last time this past fall. Making home here with financial, relationship, and conventional obligations wore us thin and repelled the man who lives on his terms.

Now, with the increased light and warmth of spring, the weight of pleasing others lifts. Now I, too, get to do what I want.

After Olivia and I squeeze each other and I show her and Patty all the goodies in the fridge for two days' meals, she waves me out of the driveway. Heading southwest with Gila wilderness topo maps, binoculars, box, and mouth and slate calls in the Tundra console and a cooler with a couple of meals and half-and-half for morning tea wedged into the back seat among the camo backpack and 20 gauge shotgun. I won't need many layers of clothing with spring weather already pushing the 80s. Down near Reserve, about four hours from Santa Fe and just east of the Arizona state line, the forecast calls for sunny skies, no wind or precipitation. I hope the ponderosa needles aren't too dry and crunchy; I'll need to be stealthy among the roost trees come dawn.

Passing through Lemitar and Magdalena, I see the draws and mesas my dog Opal and I walked for quail last winter and the seedy hotel with cardboard thin walls and flickering fluorescent lights where we stayed. Opal Luscious lay on my left in the bed, and the 16 gauge lay on my right while drunks teetered all around in the lot outside, and diesel trucks roared down US 60. Opal and I sat bolt upright in bed at 1:17 a.m. as three gunshots blasted the silence, so close I scrambled to the floor for cover, hair on end at the base of my neck.

The sheriff said, "I don't know where you come from, but around here, everyone has guns," as if to ease (or dismiss) the seriousness. He ended the conversation with, "Try to get a good night's sleep."

❦

SALTY WHITE CRUST reflects midday sun on the Plains of San Agustin, west of Magdalena. The Very Large Array, a Y-shaped configuration of twenty-seven radio antennae, each eighty-two feet in diameter, rises like awkward aliens from an otherwise iconic western landscape, interrupted by barbed wire fence lines and cud-chewing heifers. The terrain has appeared much the same since the sixteenth century when cattle and other livestock were introduced by colonial conqueror, Juan de Oñate of Zacatecas. His livestock as he left Mexico included 846 goats, 198 oxen for the carts, 2,517 sheep, 316 horses, 41 mules, 53 hogs, 500 calves, and 799 cows, steers, and bulls.

Before the Pueblo Revolt of 1680, when the indigenous people rose up against the Spanish entradas, killing at least four hundred Spaniards and running about two thousand settlers out of Pueblo territory, cattle grazed throughout the ranges of New Mexico, and the grasses provided sustenance, fattening the cattle up for profit. The conquistadores brought their own animals and their own ways of life to the west. To them, there was plenty—the land and locals would provide, even if by force.

❦

AT THE CONTINENTAL Divide Trail, I pull over and park near the horse corrals. Butterflies kick my belly into high gear as I strip off my white linen blouse, tug my Justins from my ankles and slip my jeans off. I pull on my merino wool camo shirt, stretchy camo pants, and hiking boots and sweep my hair into a tight bun. My camo cap with the face net slips on easily after three weeks of turkey hunting closer to home; it's limbered up and ready for the last weekend of the season.

I lace up my cracked hiking boots, realizing it's time for new ones. Al had purchased these for me on one of our many annual migrations to North Dakota for a summer visit with his family. Our stops in Cheyenne, Wyoming, almost always included a trip to the Sierra Trading Post outlet store. "Try these on, babe. They look like a good sturdy pair. You're going to need them." He ran his hand along the curve of my back, over my ass and down my hips as we stood at the cash register paying. "Let's go get ice cream and take a dip at Sloan Lake. They have a sweet little beach and paddle boats there," he suggested between gum smacks. Olivia perched on his shoulders, ducking beneath the doorjamb and clinging to his ears with her little mitts.

Heading into turkey country through canyon, ridge, and many oaky ponderosa slopes between Negro, Apache, Cold Springs, and Largo Canyons, I know I will stop, shift the Tundra into park, walk, and call numerous times before I reach Reserve. It's prime time, about two hours before sunset. The gobblers could be anywhere.

I take twice as long to get where I'm going; the calling takes time.

Rather than head straight to the hotel, I decide to scout the Forest Service road to the place Al has hunted for decades, where he knows the roosts and turkey routes like his own hometown. My brother Shaun and he had hunted here a few years prior, waking to gobblers practically on top of them at their campsite. Al called one in for Shaun—Shaun's first.

Driving the dusty road, gaining elevation, I peek down steep slopes, look for a pullout. At the first stop, I walk a ruddy two-track and scrape a few yelps from the box call. Nothing. I meander farther then stop. Campfire smoke alerts me to others' presence. I'm thankful for the excuse to head in a different direction. Al is everywhere. This is what he called his Honey Hole.

As I continue up the dirt road, gravel spitting from the tires into adjacent shrubbery and pinging the underside of the truck's metal frame, my calls are met with silence. No hot gobblers here tonight. It's not quite dark, so I decide to turn around and head for the sweet spot Al and I had found a few years earlier, about ten miles southwest of Reserve.

After a quick scout from the pickup through the narrow canyon near the hotel, I turn back, headlights on. Time to check in. Before hopping out of the pickup, I scan the parking lot and the surrounding buildings and highway for signs of anyone lingering, looking. I'd rather no one know what room I'm in, who's driving this vehicle, who's hunting alone 'round here.

❦

LOADED WITH COOLER, backpack, shotgun, and a bag of clothes, I push the key into the wobbly brass knob, turn it to the right and press my knee into the dark green door. The air conditioning blasts from the back corner and an American flag in whitewashed wood greets me from above the microwave where the mini coffee maker and Styrofoam cups are staged. Linoleum squeaks as I set everything down, turn the AC off and lock up behind me. No deadbolt, no security latch. The chair weighted down with my pack presses just right beneath the knob against the door.

I shower, remembering the heavy whir of the bathroom fan from my time here with Al a few turkey hunts prior. He had wrapped his body around me from the side when I came out of the shower, all shiny wet, squeaky clean. With his tongue sticking out imitating a long lick on my cheek, we took a selfie in the mirror with my phone. All grins and giggles. Turkeys brought out the silly and the wet in us.

❦

BUT AL IS long gone. Silly doesn't surface in me as easily now. I'm learning to hunt alone to follow a calling that's beyond the rational categories of food and subsistence. Centered around place, I hunt here in New Mexico, rather than accumulating trophies or faraway adventurous excursions. Here at home I build connection, belonging. Here, stepping into the hunt alone, unknowing, I detect a new self emerging unbound.

Indigenous peoples have long recognized rivers and all landscape features as literal extensions of themselves, their own bodies. This theology of place is based on a respectful, right relationship rather than consumption and extraction alone. As Gregory Cajete describes, "*Indigenous* means being so completely identified with a place that you reflect its very entrails, its insides, its soul."

The connection I crave is, perhaps, a need to realize what is indigenous in me. Not what is Native—I am white, of European descent—but what is endemic to me, inside of me, of a biology, story, and soul that are wholly me, mine. As I hunt I discover a kind of theology in my bones, my blood that expresses its long-buried religion, guiding me step-by-step through the external and internal wilds.

Who have I been all along? Can I resuscitate her here among the animals, free from anyone else's definition, dominion?

❦

BY FOUR THIRTY the next morning, I'm turning onto the Forest Service road, wishing the rumble of the engine hadn't awakened the howling dogs from the camper wedged into the furthest campsite. Looks like the guy's been there for months, electrical cords strung every which way, a solar charger set facing south, an outdoor kitchen, and gear set up like home. The dogs don't like my intrusion.

I've barely begun my ascent and the gobblers are hoppin' and calling from every direction. It's too dark to take a shot, but I still need to get to the ridge, set up and call. A few yards from where I shot the gobbler at sunrise three years earlier with Al, I set up, call, wait. After two hours of batting yelps and gobbles back and forth, the tom moves on. So do I, farther up the ridge.

I cross big turkey tracks farther up near two stock tanks. As I scan the surroundings, I find fresh sign, loads of tracks, and a handful of wing and tail feathers. They've been here.

❧

I DESCEND THE ridge, too hot to stay out and call. The gobblers are quiet, likely feeding in the canyon shadows. A nap in the air-conditioned room sounds perfect.

The gobbler approaches me, though his head and face look away. He's still alive even though he's been gutted. I have the knife in my right hand. He turns his head toward me, cranes his neck upward as if offering himself to me, surrendering his life to my hand. I feel his esophagus, his spinal cord. In this moment his body is real in my hands and also a surreal combination of a turkey's, an elk's and a human's body.

Throat. Neck. Windpipe. Esophagus. These essential elements circulate life.

His beak arches back. He breathes in deeply one last lung-full. I take my knife to his throat, feel the ridges of his windpipe, place my knife between the ridges, and slice with sure swiftness. His head wobbles loose in my left hand.

Air escapes.

In this instant the gobbler turns into a man that has a man's head and face with a baby's body. When my knife makes the cut, a tear falls from the corner of his right eye. He opens his eyes and looks at me just before dying.

He says, "I'm going now."

He inhales. His lungs fill. He brings his feet and legs up to his body like babies do, pulling into themselves.

A final exhalation escapes from the windpipe where I've made the cut. I turn my head away, not wanting to inhale anything from inside this man. I cannot take him into my body.

The deed is done. I have killed the gobbler. The baby-man is dead. The grand bird is in my hands.

I know now that it is my turn.

At 3:20 p.m., a car door slams outside, waking me to standing within seconds. A man putzes around his vehicle for about half an hour while I peek through the crimped metal blinds and get my gear on for the evening hunt.

Once he's gone, I load up and head to a different Forest Service road along a drainage off the Francisco Mountains that I spotted on the map. It looks like it may connect to the north side of the ridge where I was this morning. Maybe the turkeys are deep in, accessible to humans only by rigorous bushwhacking.

Chomping down on the last of the Chocolove almond and sea salt bar, I turn into the rutted road. Scanning the terrain, I see the area is open, less dense with trees, with more grasses that haven't been grazed to nubs yet.

Just as I turn to head up the ridge, I see turkey guts glistening red, tubular rounds, and mangled pink on the ground near the left rear tire of a parked white Chevy. A man with bloody hands steps round, feathers on his pant cuffs. "Hey! Congratulations! You got one!" I shout with an exuberant smile.

"Yep, sure did. And I worked for it, I'll tell you. Just drove in this afternoon from Rio Rancho. Thought I'd cruise around and call for a while before meeting my friend at his cabin."

"Wow, did you know about this place? Have you hunted here before?" I ask.

"Not right here, but yeah, I hunt the Gila every year. It's tradition."

"How'd you get him?" I push for more information, lapping up every detail from this fellow who seems eager to share and celebrate. He rubs his nose with his left hand, the wedding band gold squeezing a bloody finger.

"Well, when I got out and called, I heard one *waaaayyyy* up the canyon. So I got out and walked and called. Kept going toward him, calling. But then he shut up."

"They have a way of doing that. Been my experience this whole season . . . hot n' heavy then nothin'."

"Yep," he continues, "I decided to just sit and wait, be patient. Two hours passed and then he came in practically *right* on top of me. I got my gun up and *WHAM* . . . got him!"

"Good job. I'm going to turn around and get out of here so you guys can come back this evening. I've got another spot I'll try. Maybe I'll even make myself sit still."

"Good luck, ma'am. You'll get one, I'm sure!"

About twenty-five minutes later, I turn into the familiar Forest Service road where I hunted in the morning. I drive past the barking dogs, their fangs nipping my tires. The camper guy saunters out, shirtless, steps into the road behind me, follows my tracks. I see his long, dirty blonde hair, holey jeans, bare feet. His eyes are set too deep to make out. I can't tell what they're saying.

I have about three hours till dark, plenty of time to walk the ridge, call, and set up. The stock tanks higher up are the sweet spot. About halfway up the ridge, I jump from the commotion to the west. Looking through the oaks and ponderosa, I see two elk—a cow and a calf, the cow happily munching curl leaf mahogany. I get an eyeful—watch their ears twitch, the mom's hind hoof reach up to scratch, the lips curl around supple branches. The calf seems impatient, ready for the next snack stop. She looks in my direction, flares her nostrils then bolts. I'm busted.

I walk on, a little lighter on my heels. Maybe I'll get another glimpse. About two hundred yards farther, a cow stops directly in front of me in the path, spreads her back legs, tilts her head up slightly and pees. As she finishes and begins to walk east, her poop plops, one turd at a time in trail like breadcrumbs as evidence of her path. The musk consumes me, holds me there a good while. Spring feels like fall with her scent, her fresh tracks, her eyes turned to me before running over the ridge. She reminds me of the cow and bull up in Cunningham that November. Close enough to taste.

When I arrive at the tanks, I find the two feathers from the morning and push their tips into the soil at the base of a little oak behind some downfall where I'll set up. I pull the El Guique corn kernels from my inner pocket and place three at the base of the feathers. The garnet grains contrast with the humble ground.

I commit myself to this place, this lookout, until dusk. "DO. NOT. MOVE. CHRISTIE." I instruct. Usually on the move to try harder, cover ground, hunt my best, sitting still is an anomaly. I pull the camo mask down from my cap, tuck stray hair strands, and adjust the eye opening for clear visibility and place the cushion under my butt. I raise the 20 gauge to my shoulder, settle in against my pack, identify the shooting lanes—plausible openings among the brush—like Al taught me, and confirm that this is a good spot. The stock tank is visible and I have plenty of openings in multiple directions and good cover over me.

❦

OLIVIA COMES TO me as I lounge. I close my eyes, remembering the summer before when Olivia, Patty, and I camped along the

Gallina, a tributary to the Chama River near Abiquiu. We walked up the canyon with layers of Colorado red, ochre, and ash white stone walls parallel to us. Tiny figurine-like piñon and juniper perched atop the vertical walls a couple hundred feet higher, slanting north, pushed horizontal by the south winds. While I waded ankle-deep in the clay riverbed, crunched over salty edges, and called Opal off two humping lizards, Olivia ran to me, her sunbleached swimsuit dyed red from creek water, tan lines hazy where the shoulder straps had moved. With a wet red bandana tied around her little head, she made hurried tracks toward me.

"Mom! Mom! Look, look what I found!" She and Patty had explored upstream while I worked with Opal on stay, sit, come, heel. Her two palms cupped together under a tiny bird; Olivia carried her delicate find to me. Its skin was translucent, pink internal organs visible, and keratin beak newly formed. I knew what type of bird this was. "That's a turkey, sweetie. See the bands on his feathers?" The dark brown and white lines, prominent on strutting gobbler wings during mating, attract the hens as they cut showy arcs. The turkeys drag the tips in the soil, flaunting the contrast of the abstract wing pattern with the shiny gold and copper of their iridescent tails. This one probably just hatched or broke open from the safety of his egg by the previous week's monsoon flood. Cottonwood trunks and boulders still lay high and dry after the water subsided.

"Aw, Mom, he's so tiny. Look at his little feet. They're scaly, and I can sort of see his eyes." Olivia ran her fingertips over every centimeter of the chick's body, turned him gently on his back, inspecting his little pink belly, while supporting the limp neck and stroking the feathers.

"What do you think you'll do with him, hon? Do you want to put him somewhere safe?" I asked, wondering if she would want to take him home with us, cradle him on the ride back to town.

"I'm going to make something for him. Something special just for him."

She placed the turkey on a bed of cottonwood leaves and began gathering sticks, pebbles, stones and more leaves. She scoured out a dry place in the sand on the bank above the creek's high-water mark, creating a concave bowl, a soft resting place. Olivia lined the bed with leaves, three piñon jay feathers, and a wad of downy cotton from nearby. "I'll wrap him up, Mom. Like this."

Then she removed the bandana from her head, draped it in her left hand and picked up the limp gobbler from the leaves and placed him in the fabric. Crisscrossing the bandana, she folded him into the cloth and placed him in the earth coffin.

For about an hour and a half, Olivia tended to the turkey, creating a mounded grave of compacted soil and clay, embellished with nearby treasures—pine needles and cones, blue grama grass seed head, firecracker penstemon flowers, and white quartz stones. She used her palms to smooth crescents around the perimeter of the mound, pulled her fingers through the soil to ripple the edges.

"There, Mom. Do you think he'll be OK like that?"

Patty and I sat with Olivia at the grave, wondering where the other turkeys in the clutch went, how their nest fared. Did they get washed downstream too? Was the mama hen able to hang on? Did she re-nest? Did predacious birds or mammals get to them before the flood?

❦

THE SUN DIMS as the gobblers carry on. They're still interested in getting with hens. I pull off a couple more yelps, reach for my book, and check the time. Almost seven o'clock. The sweet light descends. The stock tank mirrors placid pink.

"*Putt, putt . . . putt, putt . . .*" Sounds like a hen's coming in. My heart races to attention, but I can't move. The hen is too close. I might spook her and any gobblers she's with. The book slips from my loosened grip, my legs stiffen.

Out of the corner of my left eye, I see the pale pink, whiskered head slip into view. "*Putt, putt, putt.*" She moves with caution, neck stretched long, eyes wide, scanning the area.

Knowing I can't move a muscle or even blink, I watch her move farther into the opening, her iridescent feathers catching sun's blush. At about twenty yards I see a three-inch beard and realize it's a gobbler, a young jake, not a hen as I first thought. *Shit.* I don't even have my gun up and can't move into position because I know he'll flush.

Holding as still as possible, my eyes fixate on the gobbler as he pecks and meanders around the stock tank and finally strolls off to the west behind me. Rather than accepting a missed opportunity, I lift my left thumb and forefinger to the slate call near my left thigh, gently pushing the book out of the way. I'm able to rub three faint yelps off the slate. Once, twice. I get my gun up, sit straight against the tree trunk, and take aim at the open spot.

The gobbler returns, this time with head red hot. He's looking for the hen, looking in my direction when I take the shot.

In a flailing flutter of wings, he's down on the other side of a fallen limb. Rather than risk a prolonged death or adrenaline-fueled flight, I take another shot then run over to his heaving body, shotgun lowered in my right hand.

His right cheek to the ground, left eye open, I lay my torso on top of him, knees bent at his breast. It takes all of me to still the life inside as his claws scratch for freedom, wings seek the liberty of lift-off. Holding him with my full embrace, arms wrapped around his body, my weight pressing into him, I breathe his breath, shudder his last shudder, hold him to stillness.

The other gobblers nearby continue their banter, unfazed by the ruckus. They've got hens and roosting on their minds. I set the young jake alongside my right leg as I pack up, preparing for the descent in darkness.

Shotgun over my shoulder, pack on and zipped up, and calls tucked away, I lift the bird, warm and limp, head dangling, into my arms. I cradle him down the ridge with my forearms curled up from the elbows to my biceps. He's as close as he can get, secure as I trip over roots and branches, stones, and dried cow patties. My eyes search for shadows, hints of light in the moonless sky, anything to help me find my way.

The path looks different now.

❦

THIS GILA JAKE, along with the hot gobblers in the little drainage I had hunted, are descendants not only of their turkey ancestors but also of the Gila ridges and mountains, the ponderosa, grasses, and oaks. They're descendants of the Gila River too. Undammed. Still connected. Still flowing.

Cajete describes Puebloan peoples' relationship with animals: "Animals eat other animals, and the animals that are eaten become a part of the substance of other life. Through the observation and interaction with animals over generations, indigenous people understood that animals could teach people something about the essence of transformation."

I cradle the jake, clinging to his body, hungry for something more than just his meat.

❦

MY TAILLIGHTS GLOW red against the two-dog camper's trailer. No lights there; they're all tucked in for the night. Fifteen minutes later I pull into the dirt parking lot and shut the lights and engine off. I'm alone at the hotel with no other guests, no cars, barely a sound except for the intermittent truck drumming down the highway.

The bed rests, sheets and spread tucked neatly into the mattress. The room is dark, cool, solitary. My morning teapot turned upside down to drain stains the paper towel near the sink. The day has changed me. I remove my cracked boots, laces loaded with prickly seed heads. With no one here to see or deter me, with no one else's voice yanking me toward *should*, no one else to satisfy, I allow my body to take over, no more room for reason. I lay the gobbler on the bed, his head on my pillow, his scaled feet curled along the seam in the bedspread.

His body cools, stiffens. Here in the darkness I experience an unlikely shift.

I'm here to listen. To learn. I had wanted to be good enough, an able hunter, equal to men. I had wanted to prove myself and my independent self-sufficiency. I didn't need anyone, or at least didn't want to.

But here with this gobbler, something softens, opens. If I'm gauging myself in reference to *them*, aren't I still playing by their rules, by standards I believe they have established? What would it be like now to write my own rules, try less, follow my own barometer more? Could seeking connection and learning be enough? Could kinship to place and animal be worthy goals? How could I begin to fashion new meanings and feelings of success?

I lay face-to-face with the jake, unmoving, no words through the night. The urge to get, to overcome, to know subsides. What passes between us in the dark eludes, drifts between the liminal lines of night and day like the setting moon peeking out from behind currents of clouds before daybreak. When I reach for her—grasping—her shiny womb retreats, slipping into the fold of the horizon.

TURKEY TAIL

WE STEP OUT OF our pickups to get a visual on the immediate property boundaries. "How many acres do you have here, you and your mom?" I ask the colleague of my new lover late one Sunday afternoon in May 2020 as we shake hands. The lover had called, wooing me with the offer, "Hey, Christie, my friend and his mom, Tracy, have a ranch up north. He says there are tons of turkeys there. Says you're welcome to come hunt."

I had resisted his advances, delayed responding to any texts or calls. It had been over two years since the divorce. I had finally come unwound, unbound. Single life suited me. But the opportunity to hunt turkeys on private land, where there are no other hunters and much less pressure on the birds, proved too tasty a temptation to pass up.

The plains southeast of Wagon Mound, New Mexico, break into deep canyons, ponderosa pines, and the slim ribbon of Vermejo Creek. This is the Canadian River watershed, where the water runs red, stained by the earth. The river's 906 miles connect Colorado, New Mexico, Texas, Oklahoma, and Arkansas. Even though the Canadian is dammed five times before it reaches its final destination, it meanders through extreme highs and lows from mountain summits to vegas to canyons, hydrating seed and soil and animals scaled, winged, furred, hoofed, and human.

Water doesn't speak the language of political boundaries, doesn't care about the laws around human ownership or demand.

Water curves its own course, trickles its own tongue and recedes into deep depths when overdrawn.

We stand near the pond at the Canyon House, where six narrow drainages, including Ciruela and Vermejo Creeks, converge. He shakes his head and tells me, "That's the wrong question to ask. You don't put it in number of acres, but number of head."

I resist asking more questions and let him get on with his evening as I begin shifting gears into turkey hunting mode. I only have this night and the next morning while Olivia goes to school and stays with Patty.

❦

IN 1878 AMERICAN geologist and explorer John Wesley Powell identified the one hundredth meridian west, the longitudinal line that divided the west from the east, dry from wet. West of this line, which runs straight up the Great Plains along the Texas panhandle's eastern edge through Oklahoma, Nebraska, South Dakota, North Dakota, and the Canadian province of Manitoba, was deemed too dry for agricultural production and settlement in Powell's assessment. Powell's own observations during extensive travel in the West, which took him along multiple rivers, including the Colorado, Green, and San Juan, coupled with precipitation and climate data informed his report. His extensive surveys and mapping of the West contributed to the formation of the US Geological Survey. He served as its second director. He was also instrumental in conceiving of and establishing the US Bureau of Reclamation, which oversees water resource management, in 1902.

But with the prevailing ideologies of the era—Manifest Destiny and Rain Follows the Plow—Powell's approach was ultimately rejected. Where he outlined land management plans based on watersheds and small, local community oversight, the government was more interested in identifying irrigation, cultivation, and development opportunities that would be driven by private interests and dollars. As stated in the 1912 *Quarterly Journal of Economics: Agricultural Development in the United States 1900–1910*, "Land now thought unavailable for agriculture will soon be found to be available or will be made so. Water will be drained from the land where there is too much and carried to the land where there is not enough."

Powell resigned as the US Geological Survey director in 1894. During this time and into the Progressive Era of the twentieth century, rivers were deemed "most attractive when they yielded to humanity's needs." Water became a commodity moved at will by power on paper to support agriculture, a booming mining industry, and urbanization.

❦

I HEAR THE man's pickup jiggle across the cattle guard as he leaves, and I watch the red of the truck meander a slow path through the straw-colored slopes. The herd of about twenty-five elk that has emerged from the piñon-juniper edge watches him, too, ears piqued, eyes alert. The wildlife here appears relaxed, unbothered.

The elk continue to graze, heads down, their muzzles like vacuum cleaners at earth's grassy floor. Three dainty deer prance near the elk, mule-like ears twitching and rotating to shifting sounds. I yank my jeans, white linen shirt, and cowboy boots off and pull a single layer of camo over my legs, torso, and neck. I twist my hair up into the camo cap and pull the face mask over my cheeks, finding the eye and nose holes so I can see and smell.

With one shell in the chamber and three in the magazine, safety on, and the box call in my pocket, I slither my way around the shady spring-fed pond at the foot of the house, upslope from where the turkeys have congregated.

"*Putt, putt, putt . . .*" I hear quick vocal pulses from the hens as they pluck bright green grass and watercress between their beaks, chattering and relaxed. I see three jakes, their stiff, short beards protruding perpendicular from their feathered breasts. The difference between them and the mature gobblers is evident: their heads and bodies are smaller, and the red, white, and blue of the gobblers' bulging crowns, snoods, dewlaps, and caruncles are visible at a glance, whereas the jakes' heads have fewer definitive features and are smaller and gray. The jakes take their cues from the hens.

I'm about thirty feet away, my back held straight by the massive cottonwood trunk, its craggy bark snagging the thin merino wool of my camo top. While I listen to the gals, I watch the jakes, itching to take aim before sundown. The three juvenile males opt for a curious detour around the fence line and, with a raucous flutter of heavy wings, they launch themselves into the cottonwood I'm leaning against. They perch and preen themselves on three lateral branches about twenty feet above me.

As darkness settles and the hens, too, situate themselves in their arboreal resting roost, I lower the shotgun, stretch my legs, and relax. The turkeys' scaled claws scratch the limbs overhead, shadows of fluffed bodies loom above me, and an occasional tail ruffle interrupts the quietude as stars emerge.

Suddenly the ground rumbles beneath me. About five horses thunder so close I wonder if they'll run me over. But at about ten feet, they stop, snort, swish their long, untamed tails, and stare, nostrils raised high trying to make sense of the strange intruder. We hold each other's gazes, motionless. They rush off whinnying with abrupt intensity. I stand, stretch, and make my way back to the pickup with the turkeys tucked in for the night.

❦

THE WAXING GIBBOUS moon keeps me awake. I lay in the bed of my pickup, tucked into thick blankets and sleeping bags while the bloated celestial body presses into me, round, golden. I toss and turn through the night. Before pulling away from the hunting ground just after sunset, I witnessed two young, antlerless elk standing tall on their hind legs, their front legs pawing at each other in what looked like a playful sparring match. I imagine them now alternating elevated paw prance play with practical grazing.

I envision the turkeys and wonder if the moon illuminates their iridescent feathers. Could I see more than their silhouettes if I crept down beneath the cottonwood again? Would they be making different middle-of-the-night sounds that I've never heard? I want to know the language of the moon, the meaning of turkey tongue, the messages of elk tracks pressed into wet mud. Which way do they go and why? My words and ways of making meaning seem so dull, flat, one-dimensional. Isn't there something more than the rationale of the human mind? The questions lull me to sleep, for a suspended moment, between earth and moon.

I walk alone. A kestrel flies in front of me. She has caught a little sparrow and is trying to eat her in midflight. The little bird flaps its wings, desperate to escape the hooked beak, the razor claws.

It flaps free for a split second and gets caught in my hair. I feel it flailing, panicking in the unfamiliar terrain of human hair.

The wing beat is right in my ear. It can't find its way free.

I tousle the strands with my hands trying to liberate the bird, my right ear filling with its flapping. I can't shake it loose.

I bend over with an exaggerated WHOOSH, releasing my hair to the ground. I shake it wild from my neck. I look up from the ground, upside down, at my hair. I touch it with my hands. The bird is still there, stuck.

I touch my locks again, trying to feel the little life so stubbornly embedded there.

But I no longer feel hair. The material and texture between my fingers are feathers. Long, cascading layers of feather after feather. Banded copper, iridescent blue, green, rich brown, tiny white fringe.

In that moment, the bird is set free. My turkey tail fan spreads wide, releases the sparrow.

The bulging brightness of the moon grows weightier as I come to, wide eyed beneath her. I finally surrender. I stop trying to sleep and decide to absorb the starry screen above, try to make myself nocturnal too. Maybe I can wish upon a shooting star or receive some sort of vision from the heavenly bodies that tells me how to be a good hunter tomorrow. What would the land say if we spoke the same tongue? Would the Vermejo Creek spill herself open to me?

A west wind tousles my hair and rattles the nylon lawn chair. The elk, turkeys, deer, cottonwoods, and the creek cast their dreams to the moonlight.

❦

"WE'RE ABOUT FIFTY to sixty years behind in understanding what our underground water resources are," Kate Zeigler, owner and senior geologist at Zeigler Geologic Consulting, tells me over the phone. "We've been working in Union County and other places in the state and in Colorado and Oklahoma to help landowners understand what is invisible below ground."

Ziegler consults with rural communities and agricultural producers about groundwater resources and has worked with the Northeastern Soil and Water Conservation District to monitor groundwater volume and health since 2010. In 2014 she started working with the Mora-Wagon Mound Soil and Water Conservation District and met Tracy, the woman who had settled in and learned cattle, ranching, and rural New Mexico life nearly fifty years ago through trial and error along with generous guidance from the locals.

"These people know their land better than I ever will. They've lived here their whole lives. I'm trying to provide the scientific data that tells the story of what's happening down deep, why wells aren't pumping as much or are drying up. We're trying to adapt to changing weather patterns and the fact that aquifers aren't recharging like they used to," Zeigler explains. "Groundwater is invisible so you can't see when the tank is low. But we can at least measure the bottom of the well and the rate of decline, so folks know how much time they have."

She says that among the seven counties and five hundred wells they're monitoring, 85 percent of those wells are not recharging within a human lifetime.

❦

THE MOON SETS to the west. I rise, sit with the morning silence, and sip my creamy Earl Grey, itching to get going. I'm up a good two hours before daylight, well before the turkeys will take flight from their roosts. Maybe I'll head down to the spring early and get set up, listen for new turkey talk at daybreak, and be in the best position to take aim once they're on the ground.

I drive the pickup down the meandering dirt road, over the cattle guard, and follow the creek in. No elk. No deer. No horses. There are a couple of smaller cottonwoods north of the main roost tree. I set up against the base of one and swing the 20 gauge around in a 180-degree swath, making sure I have as many shooting lanes as possible. The spring water illuminates dawn light in a dappled, watery mirage.

Just when there's enough sunlight to make out silhouettes, another rumbling like last night's quakes beneath me. The little herd of horses rushes toward me. I strain my eyes, noticing something different. There is a new shape now, a slight, wobbly four-legged foal with a sprightly, swishing tail.

The mare with the low, swollen belly who met me at the cattle-guard the evening before gave birth during the night. The little one holds my stare as the sun rises and the turkeys descend.

❦

IN AN INSTANT, all hens and jakes scatter, heading down the valley, across the fence, and toward the neighboring property. They did not do what I expected and are all now far beyond shooting range. I reach for the box call and whip off a few hen yelps to try to lure the jakes back. One stops, turns, listens, and gobbles. I watch him putter around, pecking at the ground and looking for the hen. I call once more, wait for him to turn his head, and then lower myself to the ground and crawl closer.

He gobbles again, fluffs his wings, and fans his tail. There's a pile of slash wood in the middle of the field that I crawl behind, about fifty yards from him. On my knees, I pull another call and watch him do something unlikely: he bends down and pushes himself beneath the lowest strand of barbed wire, coming closer to find the mystery hen that keeps calling.

Once he comes within the thirty-yard range, I rise to my knees, swing the shotgun toward him, and fire.

❦

"WHAT'S CHANGING? I mean how are folks adapting to less water and more unpredictable weather?" I ask Kate.

"Well, they're now shutting wells off after the cattle have been shipped away, rather than running them year-round. They've also experimented with less water-intensive crops like milo or feed-grade corn. It all depends on the fluctuation of crop prices. They've got to plant what they need to make enough money for their families."

Kate goes on, "In addition to managing water on the ground, there's policy and different stakeholders. There's so much distrust among groups and some talking down to others thinking they—the politicians or the scientists—know better. But really, all of us need to come to the table. We try to get the data into the landowners' hands so that they can at least be part of the conversation."

When I press further about how much time there is left, Kate doesn't give a definitive answer. I know the question is loaded and that each well, aquifer, and ranch is different.

She pauses then says, "These people are family to us now. We get upset when things happen out there. I tell them, 'We will be with you to the bitter end, until the last drop. We're with you.'"

❧

AFTER THE TURKEY has been hit and tumbles, his right wing curves skyward, his feet pedal slowly as if trying to find stable ground again. I go to him, put the shotgun down, and place the weight of my body on his. His breathing lifts my torso slightly. He blinks, breathes, and blinks one last time. His final flutter ripples through me as I, too, exhale. The ranch awakens to daylight. The spring lies still, reflecting the cottonwood branches above.

I hoist the jake over my right shoulder and head up the slope to slice him open and extract the guts. After two steps I see what looks like a large, shiny, white and red plastic bag in front of me. My first thought is trash, which I'm used to seeing strewn all over public land. But upon closer inspection, I realize it's the afterbirth of the foal, where the mare labored the night before, just ten feet from where this turkey died.

❧

WITHIN SIXTEEN HOURS I bear witness to death and birth, to wildlife congregating to drink at the bank of quiet water, to sun and moon cycles. Many beings of this Wagon Mound place have danced within a relationship of extremes, where water gives and takes.

Thankful for the rare access to private land and the fairytale-like hunt, I call the lover, "Hey, I wanted to let you know I had an amazing time. I'm coming home with a young gobbler. I'll bring you some broth. Maybe we can cook over a fire."

I know he's not Al. I know the hunt, the harvest, the trekking and tracking aren't his language. But he's an artist, a father, a builder. His ambition and creativity sweep me away. His hazel brown eyes and sun-bleached brown curls soften my resolve. Maybe we can make a go of it. Maybe I can stoke the flames with this man, get a love burning hot, a love that fuels new possibility.

I'm thankful for the two-hour drive to Santa Fe. I don't want to let go of the elk, deer, newborn foal, or the moon. I want to take what I've learned from the spring with me: slow down, meander and recharge down deep.

The seat next to me holds an unlikely passenger. The jake rests, stiffening with each hour past death. His claws curl, cold. No branch to grip now. I get to see him up close, his feathers with iridescent shine and fine fringe. I resist the urge to call Al, to rattle off the story of the hunt. I resist the urge to head north on the interstate, through the Great Plains toward that faraway place Al drifted. Instead I navigate toward Olivia and Opal, toward home.

Once back at the house, I will lay the turkey on the cutting counter to skin and butcher. I will stretch his pelt wide, fanning his wings and tail and salt the underside, then pin him to the board where he'll dry in the security of the shed over the coming year.

The warm internal organs I tugged from the young gobbler's core rest atop the smooth boulder west of the Canyon House. Which scavenging birds and mammals will become turkey tonight? What of him will they taste and carry inside their own bodies? Will the Vermejo and Ciruela linger above ground long enough to quench future thirsts? How will my own cravings be satisfied?

❦

ONCE BACK IN Santa Fe, I get to Olivia's school in time to peek into the dance studio. She doesn't see me behind the black velvet curtain. Ms. Rozann, her ninety-year-old ballet teacher with pearls draped at the basin in her collar bone, instructs, "Olivia, you've got to lift that leg. Let the air be your joy. Don't work it with muscle or might. Smile, darling."

Olivia creases her brow, trying not to try.

We arrive home at suppertime and agree that a meal of biscuits appeals the most. "Let's eat on the portal and cool off. Looks like it might rain. Clouds are rolling in from the east, thunder too. Maybe we'll get some moisture after this dry spell."

❦

THE SANTA FE River, whose headwaters originate east of the city at Lake Peak's 12,408 feet and run forty-six miles to the confluence with the Rio Grande near Cochiti Pueblo at 5,220 feet, carries water, silt, asphalt residue and debris from its 285-square-mile watershed. The river has known many lives, flowing wet to dry over the centuries since the Puebloans planted crops at its shore and the conquistadores imposed strict orchard rows and corralled domestic animals.

Today the river runs at its fullest from spring snowmelt runoff that flows from the McClure and Nichols dams and reservoirs. The urban waterway hydrates habitats, wildlife, recreation, and agriculture. I've found pottery sherds on our two-acre property that once was Tewa land, on the banks of the river, about twenty miles from the river's headwaters. Puebloans made home here centuries ago. They knew where life was wettest.

"The elders watched clouds day in and day out. Centuries of such observations permitted them to discern the relationships and characteristics of clouds. They recognized all types of rain that would be possible from particular types of clouds. Whether snow, sleet, wind with rain, baby rain, grandfather rain, or mother rain, they honored the kinds of rain that brought them life," Gregory Cajete stories bodies of water as learned and revered lineage.

There was no separation between clouds and rain or between the rain and the creek or the creek and the river. All water is connected, circular, cyclical. Disconnect between the people and the water would be disrespectful, even deadly, as would disconnect among the sources and types of water.

❦

OLIVIA FINISHES OFF the dishes—licking peach jam from the plate before plunging it into soapy water—while I return calls from afternoon messages.

"Mom, I wanna show you the dance we learned today. Come on!" Olivia twirls out the sliding glass door to the portal, her feet circling like the bundles of wheat in the wind overhead. Corn stalks stand tall in the garden beds flanking the portal. They dry in the late summer heat. This is the first time I've planted the corn seed from El Guique.

"Honey, I can't dance. You know that. I don't have a dancing bone in my body. I'd be best left to keeping the beat with my foot on the ground," I apologize, sorry I can't meet her in her grace, her passion.

"Like this . . ." she lifts my hands, palm to palm, guiding me round and round, the south and west portal concrete our dance floor. I finally let myself go, laugh, see the sun setting in Olivia's green eyes. It feels good to be young again.

Olivia heads back in as night falls. Tomorrow is Friday. I'll finish cutting the turkey, salting his skin and securing him in the shed, away from flies and critters.

But now, the rains are coming. I turn the porch light off, pull off my Justin boots, unbuckle my belt, remove my jeans and white linen shirt. I push them aside with my bare toes, peeking out the driveway to see if any neighbors are coming. As I tiptoe down to the river, the clouds ahead let loose. I can tell this is a grandmother rain, a soft, wet, warm one whose water kneads the crusted earth. We've been thirsty for too long.

Unlatching the gate, I cross the gravel path and descend along the river's bank. The willows brush my calves, find their way between my naked thighs to another type of wetness. My arms push cottonwood branches aside, and broad leaves slap me in the face, teasing me to smile.

I see the water coming. She's flowing downstream, finding her way to me, her belly slithering silver across sand. Her first wave, like a flickering tongue, traces a new path over dry ground. The dams let loose, can't contain her volume, her power any longer.

My hair hangs heavy, weighted with rain, rivulets trail down my spine, between my breasts. My eyes take me higher, looking to the stars emerging from the new moon sky. I can see them defying city lights . . . Can they see me?

Spinning round and round, my feet press into wet clay, water swirls around my toes. The earth is thick enough here to hold my print, a haphazard, illogical path beaten in place by heart rhythms.

I look down, try to trace my path back home. Olivia will wonder where I've been.

But all I see are symmetrical, semicircle points pressed among the stones, padded paw prints and claw marks, a triple-toed, scaled scratch. The rain pools in the tracks, gathers wet, making moist ground for new seeds.

WANING

Last lunar phase. Sunlit portion of the moon decreases significantly.

Only a select segment is visible.

She curls inward.

DREAM CYCLES

REM and NREM sleep alternate throughout the night in ninety-minute intervals.

Later at night, toward morning, NREM cycles shorten while REM cycles lengthen.

Between dark and light, sleep deepens, dreams intensify.

2020–2021

LITTLE BULL

I ENTER THE HOUSE of my elder friend Rose. We met in January 1998 when I moved to Santa Fe. She shook my hand then, but her eyes were the real greeting. Warm and knowing, she held my gaze, lingered there as if trying to locate something inside me. She lived between worlds, old and new, primal and modern. She was more moon than sun, and the dream was her domain.

Now I see her round table centered in the living room, situated low to the floor. There is a silk cloth covering the circular altar, and its pale floral pattern softens the surroundings. Rose sits cross legged on the plush rug. This is her place of reverence and ritual.

As I stand there observing the table and Rose, she smiles and laughs with a childish chuckle, then spins the table like a wheel of fortune.

She spins it counterclockwise.

"See Christie, do the circumambulation in reverse. Go ahead. I know, I know, at the Zen center we always did walking meditation clockwise. And people always go with a clock flow of time. But now it's OK to go in reverse. Try it. Just this once."

She keeps laughing. Her body shakes with joy and tears burst from the corners of her eyes.

I consider the possibility of reversing my planned route. What if I begin in the east and move west? What if I move like the moon?

Today is the opening day of the elk hunt in Unit 51, where I hunted elk alone for the first time during a new moon two years ago, when the elk were everywhere but I never took a shot. I choose to return here, to pick up from where I left off and see whether this time I can make the connections. Maybe this time it will all come together—me, the elk, the bullet. This morning the weather has shifted. The wind howls, snowflakes flurry in every direction, and heavy gray clouds obscure the sun.

I wear extra layers knowing that the temperature will hover in the twenties, knowing that the wind will whisk away all warmth from the sun.

I start out backward today like Rose suggested, last night's dream still at the surface, within reach. "OK," I tell myself, "Let's go in from the top and work our way down."

I take a few steps, stop, look through the binoculars, and take a few more steps. The sun hasn't risen, but the binos allow for close-up inspection of shadows and movement. Details emerge when I slow down. Fresh tracks and scat appear. A broken branch I hadn't noticed yesterday when I was scouting dangles, barely hanging on by the thin skin of craggy bark as if someone had snapped it over a knee. I stop, scan, listen, step, repeat. The gray jay adds levity to the murky morning. She alights as I step, lands as I pause. Her mini toes curl around the bare sliver of a dead spruce branch. I see her seeing me. Her glass eyes peer into mine as if she's asking for explanation, the why behind which way I choose to go. Little does she know I would trust her instruction more than my own.

By 7:00 a.m. daylight exposes the ground. I see yesterday's tracks and those from days before. I see my route behind me, trace the rhythm of the search for the last thirty minutes. A wisp of hair escapes the tuck of my wool cap, tickles my cheek. The weather is shifting, and clouds obscure the hint of sun that tried to peel the horizon line. Today there will be blustery snow.

I remove my pack, unbutton my wool pants, push my long johns down my legs, and squat to pee. Steam rises. No blood this time, though my period often begins on the first day of the hunt. Now

I'm ovulating. The left side of my lower abdomen is tender, swollen. When my boots contact the earth, a minor twinge of pain erupts from my ovary, as if the walking will shake the tiny egg of hopeful life loose. For as long as I can remember, my menstrual cycles have followed the moon but fluctuated seasonally. During the summer months I bleed when the moon is full. In winter I flow during the new moon. Spring and fall are in-between times of transition. Now I'm midcycle, hungry to make life. I imagined this would have subsided before I turned fifty, that my body would let go of her urge to propagate, to be fecund, wet, and pulsing with an urgency to make babies.

I secretly covet the rhythms, changes, and cycles, like I have my own kind of deep moon inside, waxing and waning, a push-pull of tides coaxing the flow of richness toward and away from estrus. I'm greedy for the extremes.

Buckling back up, I look at the dark north wood about fifty yards in front of me. My gut knows this is where I must go. I know this is the direction of the counterclockwise first steps I must take. I tremble and finally say out loud what shakes me from the inside: "I'm scared."

I hold still, inhale then exhale.

"Scared of what?" I whisper under my breath to myself, allowing the question to percolate then surface.

"Getting lost."

But I know there's something deeper than these surface fears.

"Scared of what?" I ask again, this time louder. My voice penetrates the silence, whirs with the wind.

What if I do make the shot and she bolts? What if I can't find her and she's out there injured, suffering? What if I don't know how to make the cuts? What if I can't haul her out on my own? What if I'm lost, unable to navigate the terrain out there or the terrain of doubt inside?

I inhale again, open my lungs and belly, stand straighter. Incidents from the past two hunts surface, vivid.

"Christie, your feet are in such bad shape, I'm afraid you won't be able to pack her out if you get one," the man spoke through the phone, long distance. He was the first someone new after Al. He had hunted most of his life and lived and worked in the Wisconsin forests every day. His calm, even temperament and grown-up wholeheartedness appealed to me in contrast to Al's wild impulses.

"Let me think about it. I'll let you know," I responded, knowing I didn't want him or anyone with me on the upcoming hunt but wondering if I should accept his expertise and help. Maybe I did need backup this time . . .

Earlier that fall I accepted his invitation to come hunt whitetail deer with him and his close family and friends at The Shack in Wisconsin, a long-standing community hunting tradition. I would be the first outsider to be included. Once there, "Just shoot," advice came at me from all the guys. This was different country unlike the more open terrain of New Mexico that afforded better sight lines to take aim. The north Wisconsin woods were dense with aspen thickets and masses of understory. The deer would not be easy to see, let alone shoot.

"But what if I can't see the vital zone? I don't want to make a mess of the killing," I asked. Still, they encouraged me to take the shot no matter what, to simply pull the trigger and fire into the forest as best I could. They wanted me to get what I came for. Surely their clear directives would bolster my confidence.

We would be hunting from stands secured to trunks of trees about ten feet above ground. I had only done this once before, this kind of sitting, watching, and waiting from an elevated advantage. This place, this man, and this way were all new.

On opening morning, the man, his brother, his daughter, and I headed toward our separate stands. My boots squeaked through icy snow in step with a wolf who had walked this way about a day earlier. I stopped, sized up my footprint against hers, and lingered there, absorbing this unfamiliar predator in whose home I, too, would be hunting. Was she watching me from the timbers now? Would her howl beckon the moon forth come sundown. Maybe she would track me then, on my way out.

I climbed up the stand, shifting the bulk of my thick layers of wool and blaze orange overcoat, adjusting the sling of the rifle to insure it wouldn't slip as I ascended the metal steps. Once situated with the safety bar in place, the man turned and left with, "Good luck. Shoot straight."

Three hours later, after alternating episodes of glassing, dozing, and trying to stay warm, I got down to pee. As I buttoned up my wool pants and cinched the belt, I saw deer eyes and ears at about seventy-five yards. The rest of her body was completely obscured. As I scrambled to get the Mauser in position and focus the scope, no part of me felt ready to pull the trigger, but "just shoot" penetrated my doubt. I went for it.

SLAP! The deer dropped as the bullet penetrated her flesh, but her head was still up. Moving toward her with my gun ready, I prepared for the next shot, but she darted off. There where she fell, warm blood melted hollow holes into the snow.

Rather than chase her farther into the forest, I climbed the stand, watched and listened. I remembered Al's instruction from years ago in the Vermejo. I made myself wait.

The two men came after hearing my shot, "Good job, Christie! Let's go find her."

"Right there," my friend said. "You can see that it's her rear right leg that's injured. That's where she laid down." He deciphered details I hadn't learned to read yet. All I saw was compacted snow and blood. About one hundred yards beyond, as the three of us approached a willowy wetland, we heard labored snorting, like an exaggerated exhale, "*HUFF HUFF.*" She was bedded down but stood up when we neared.

"Take another shot!" my friend instructs.

Again, barely able to make out the form of the deer, I pull the trigger. She drops at last.

"Good job, good job!" The guys reach for a fist bump, a hand-shake, a hug. I fold down next to her, remove my gloves and stroke her flanks, run my fingers down her slim ankles. I see now that this is a young buck, with barely formed nubs as emergent antlers.

"Look here, smile. Let me get a photo," the prospective partner says.

"No, please, no photos."

After I've field dressed the deer, the partner offers to drag him out through the trees and to the pickup. "No, it's OK. I've got him," I reply, pulling the tow strap that's wrapped around his back ankles over my right shoulder. I want to feel the weight of the deer as part of my own body. I want to earn the gift of his life through my labor. I shepherd him through his north woods, where I am a visitor.

❦

HERE, NOW, EVEN in the familiar terrain of New Mexico meadows and mixed conifer forests, a messy shot that injures an elk could be too much for me to handle. I doubt I would have located that deer if not for the two men more experienced than me in following up the shot. Would I have been able to shoot, track the wounded animal, and take him down on my own?

To loosen the fear and dispel the rerun of the Wisconsin hunt, I tell myself out loud, "Well then, how about we just take one baby step at a time? How about if you feel too scared to go on, we turn back. We can always go back." These words surface as they would if I were assuring Olivia. I imagine my hand at the small of her back, holding her spine, steady.

"Ok, then. One step at a time. OK, I'll try it," I convince myself out loud. "Remember, there's fresh snow. So walk where you can see where you've walked." This guidance percolates from within, moves my lips almost involuntarily. The riddle of this koan coaxes me, my mouth making words like practical marching orders. "Walk where I see I have walked," I breathe into the swirl of snow. I hear my voice open the hush that cloaked the shadowy trees.

Step one.

Step two.

Step three.

The crusty snow crunches beneath my boots, rubbery soles press on. Within five minutes I'm deep into the blackness of dense spruce. Fallen trees in all directions make walking in a straight line impossible. I lift my knees over the crisscrossed branches, sloughing bark as the toe of my boot skims the arc of heavy trunks. I shift the weight of my rifle, heave my pack more securely onto my shoulders, and scan for movement ahead.

❦

ROSE SMILES, NODS to me like a soft mother encouraging the toddler to stand and feel her new, upright way of moving through the world. She laughs again, "That's right, like that, just like that . . ." reaching her open palms toward me.

I listen to Rose this time. I try a new way that attunes to a different, internal core. Trusting this new step-by-step, counterclockwise approach, I allow a slower pace where curiosity—rather than intensity—guides. Weather sinks in and darkens what should be dawn.

Time ticks. The day opens.

More flakes drift and begin to accumulate on last week's crusted base. The shifting wind decreases my chances of sneaking up on the animals. Surely, they'll smell me even if the sound of my boots breaking through the snow doesn't give me away. The forest closes behind me, and the spruce ghosts murmur low moans. Clouds have thickened since I entered, and shadows become less distinct. Muted light blurs outlines. I look back more often, wondering if accumulating snow will obscure my prints, erase my way back.

Just as I commit to going deeper in, continuing my gentle descent into thicker trees, they appear. The cow elk—one, two, three, maybe four—move in methodical horizontal motion against the whimsical snow flurry cascade, like a silken scarf pulled between the vertical trunks, nearly imperceptible waves of motion. They're barely visible for the dense tree trunks and dim light and the flakes that cluster on my eyelashes, obscuring my view. But I see the cows' wide ears, thick auburn necks, and slender tawny ankles. They move like a collective apparition, muzzles tugging at dormant wisps of grass through the matte white crust. They're within range at about one hundred yards.

I move into action as my body overtakes my mind. Crouching down, I position the shooting sticks in front of me and place the rifle at the crotch of the support. Looking through the scope, I place the crosshairs on one elk then the other, but there's no clear shot. Too much timber. I wait and look, holding in deep breaths to calm my nerves. If the one cow in the middle takes two more steps to the east, I'll have a shot. I release the safety, move my index finger toward the trigger, and prepare to exhale with the squeeze, but my knees shake, and the ground thunders. Just as I look in the direction of the uproar, another elk runs at me, the momentum of her speed pushing her full force in my direction. We lock eyes, my shock meeting hers. She slams on the brakes, locks her front legs, and pushes her heavy hooves to a hard stop. The whiff of her musk floors me. I hold my body tight, brace for a collision. She is only about ten feet away, but in an instant she turns, bolts in the opposite direction, and disappears.

I hold steady, my knees and breath trying to find each other.

The other elk have moved on.

❧

"OK, I GUESS it probably is a good idea for you to come on down. If I'm lucky enough to get an elk, I would want to pack her out myself. But you're right, I may not be able to," I tell the man when I call him back.

My feet had deteriorated in the months after the divorce. Opal and I walked each day for miles in the Caja west of the house, pounding cross-country, each step a sort of rhythmic command to let Al go, to move forward, find my future. The weeks and months and miles pressed on, my feet bearing too much each day. I wore them out trying to out-walk the pain.

Once at the hunting lodge on the private ranch, the man and I enter just after sunset. The ranch owner, guides, and hunters from west Texas gather around the dining table. I'm not a guest paying for a full-service, guided hunt, but I have to check in each day to confirm my designated hunting area.

"Are you one of the hunters?" I ask a rotund, rosy-cheeked man sitting by the stone fireplace.

"I wouldn't call myself a hunter, exactly," he bellows, "I'm a *shooter!* Not so interested in the hunting part."

Everyone laughs.

I'm starting to get the picture: the guides chauffeur the guests on four wheelers to the shooting spot, where they know the elk will be. This way there is no walking, no effort or actual hunt involved. The guests who've paid high dollar can easily score the elk and then have fully processed, packaged meat shipped to their door back home.

"Well, good luck out there!" I muster some cheer, turn, and head back to the Airstream to get set up, warm the green chile stew, and scour the maps.

"Let's make a plan." the partner suggests. "Fail to plan, and plan to fail!" he gleams. I can tell he has a prescribed method, that he wants this to be successful in the ways he knows have worked in the past.

I bristle, resisting a collaborative, step-by-step, formulaic way. I study the maps and familiarize myself with the terrain, but I prefer instinct as guide.

❦

WITH THE STICKS folded and tucked in the strap of my backpack and the rifle slung over my right shoulder—safety on—I tiptoe to the place the elk had just been. Like an intruder at a family gathering, I trace their tracks and look for clues of how many were there and where they ate, peed, pooed. I veer slightly to the left and see compressed melted snow in the shape of their bellies and legs bent underneath them—a bedding area where three or four had gathered in quiet respite. I kneel, touch my index and middle fingers to the smooth depression, trace the lines where rigid hooves had stood before settling into rest. Fresh yellow pee stains like holes drilled into crusty snow and greasy green oval turds release their scent.

I linger here in the bedroom of the elk, low down in the tangled forest. I've watched them before in places like this where they're at rest, their eyes low, lashes tickling their cheeks as they doze. The elk know when to charge uphill and when to rest, when to conserve their energy. Ears twitch and turn, shifting orientation to various sounds. One cow is always on watch, looking out for the herd. She's slightly more awake than the others, at ease midmorning after grazing through the night and into dawn.

The snow stiffens as temperatures drop. Snowflakes accumulate on the brim of my wool hat and in the folds of my backpack. The breeze picks up and the sky darkens. The clouds press down on me as if tapping their finger on the face of a watch. Weather is creeping in.

I whisper the mantra, "One baby step at a time," tracing the tracks of the cow elk heading east. Rather than a straight line, a succession of hoof prints, there are prints on prints, a mosaic mess that looks like a party got busted and everyone went in all directions at once. I pick a pair and follow them, downslope, farther into the dark wood.

The denser the downed trees and thick slash, the less likely my chances are of getting close to them again. They're well on their way to the day's hideout somewhere out of reach.

I hang back, turn, and recalibrate to a different tack. Moving west toward the route I was originally planning to take, I ease my grip on the rifle sling, loosen my lower jaw and soften my eyes.

❦

ON THE SECOND morning of that private ranch hunt with the Wisconsin man after a day with no elk and the delay of having to shovel out from being stuck in snow drifts, the partner and I head to newly assigned territory. As we traversed an open meadow, high noon sun melted snow from conifer branches. Glistening drops hung from the prickly needles. Rather than continuing north, I was drawn east into the oak brush. Within a few hundred yards, I spotted a spike bull. Motioning to the partner with my index finger over my mouth and the other fingers upright above my head, I let him know the elk was right there. I sank to my knees, looked through the binos, and prepared to set up and shoot. I figured the rest of the herd was near.

The spike moved upslope toward a brushy ridge, other blonde rumps in steady succession. Unable to make out how many or their sex, I took off in pursuit, pushing up the rocky slope through fresh snow. I assumed the partner trailed me as support, but he had elected to lag behind, to not get in the way.

I tracked the elk, touched tufts of their hair caught on rough bark, mashed their slippery turds between my fingers, and inhaled their scent, electrified by its immediacy. I was so close but not close enough.

Cresting the slope, I saw one herd to the east and one to the south. I straddled the barbed wire fence, climbed over, and crept to cover, trying to stay downwind and out of sight. They were at ease, heads down, grazing. Looking through the binos, I decided on a cow that was slightly separate from the others. After setting up on my belly, rifle resting on my pack on a fallen log, I took aim and pulled the trigger. Without another steady set of eyes to focus on the animals through binoculars, without a backup witness, I couldn't tell if the shot had made contact. I shot again, believing I was aiming at the same elk that I had missed before. The elk held. None bolted, none fell. Was there a dead elk? A wounded elk? Or had I missed completely? Trying to gather composure, to be sure, to "just take the shot," I fired again. And again, like the Texans the day before when I heard eight rounds up the meadow from our afternoon sit spot.

"Eight shots? Who in the hell needs eight shots?" I had asked, as if that would never happen to me, as if I'd make a clean kill with one or two rounds—or choose not to shoot at all.

But here in the confused frenzy of clustered elk on a slope, without the benefit of a spotter next to me, and my own doubt fueled by the tug of war between how the men do it and how I want to do it, I fired. And kept firing. Still no downed elk.

When the elk eventually spooked and took off, I ran to where they had been, searching for clues, drops of blood, or any sign that I'd made the hit. A couple of hours passed; daylight waned. No elk. No man. I had fired multiple other times to signal my whereabouts, but I was on my own, with no maps or food and only about half a bottle of water left.

I had handed over the necessities for him to carry. He had everything in his pack, so I knew better than to attempt a cross-country trek in the dark. If I lost my way, no one could find me out there at night.

I chose the Forest Service roads as my route, even though the distance back to the truck would far exceed a more direct path from where I shot to where we had parked that morning, which was probably three miles at most if walked in a straight line.

A few more hours and about ten circuitous miles later, as I rounded the last bend toward the Tundra, my last sip of water drained from my bottle, two guys in a pickup rolled to a stop, "Hey, are you with that guy up there? The one in the Tundra?"

"Yes! Yes! Is he there? How do you know?" I pant, fatigue blurring my words, intensifying my desperation.

"We just saw him with the door open. The cab light was on," the guys assured.

"Oh, thank goodness. It's just a little way farther." I exhale, press on.

Ten minutes later, when I arrive at the clearing, there is no pickup. No man. No shelter. He left. He took the truck, the food, and the water and was gone.

By then, my feet were already past the point of pain, past the damage from cumulative overuse and "the worst case of plantar fasciitis I've ever seen" per the local podiatrist. But there was no other option but turn, backtrack, and head toward camp, at least five miles farther down the canyon.

Robotically I slogged over my mushy tracks in the thick mud that hardened with each hour past sunset. I chose not to light the way with my headlamp, but to rely on the hint of moonlight rising in the east. I could just make out the deep ruts, the edges of snow and meadow, the surest route down to safety. My pack and rifle dug into my shoulders. My hips were numb from bearing the pack weight. My feet had long since checked out, marching on by will alone.

"Keep going. Don't stop. Walk, Christie, keep walking," I told myself.

At eight thirty, about seven hours after we got separated, I heard a vehicle approaching, saw headlights from behind casting the shadow of my body onto the road. I was nearly back to camp, having descended from the high hunting grounds. I knew there was one more curve and a slight descent until I could see the lights of camp.

He approached, slowed to a stop. Said he went looking for me. Didn't know. Thought I was coming back. Thought he was doing the right thing.

"Never. Ever. Take the vehicle. It is home base. It is what stays, always, where we left it. Never take what's safe and leave the other person without. I thought this was a given. Thought you knew this basic rule. Thought you knew better." I seethed, barely able to look him in the eye. Something in me wanted to make him the enemy, to prove myself right, that *they* were indeed the bad guy.

Once in the passenger seat, heater cranked up, silence hanging heavy between us, I heard a loud hissing sound. When I rolled down my window, I realized the right rear tire was spewing air. It had been punctured.

"Must have happened when I went looking for you. I shouldn't have gone on that rocky back route. It was barely even a road. Bet I scraped the tire there," he apologized.

What I had feared from hunting alone, what I imagined I couldn't or wouldn't know how to handle contrasts with what feels like the liability of this man. Couldn't I just fix the tire myself, get in, drive to camp, sip tea, eat supper, and then rest—alone? Could I leave him behind now too?

❧

I CONTINUE THROUGH the spruce and aspens, their trunks squeaking and swaying like tired old men shifting weight on stiff hips. The wind has picked up, gusting to at least thirty miles per hour. Trees creak and groan, and finally, at peak wind around mid-morning, I decide the safest move is no move. I bend my knees, slide my back down an aspen that's at least eighteen inches in diameter. The solid, rooted mass anchors me as I recall Rose again.

❧

WITHIN A FEW months of arriving in Santa Fe when I was twenty-seven, Rose had been there as I embarked on a group wilderness fasting retreat. We were to spend four days and nights without food or shelter, alone on the red rock mesas north of Abiquiu. One-on-one with Rose the evening before departure, I confided in her, asking, "What if I can't do it? What if something happens to me out there?"

"Christie. You will be alright. Remember, when you're feeling scared, when you've lost yourself, just lie down. Put your whole body on the earth. She is always there, holding you. Let her. She is that big."

❦

LIKE THE SHATTERING crack of fireworks, the trees begin to snap and fall, the weight of holding on surrenders to a wind that knows the trees' weakness: years of drought have worn the forest down, shriveled the layers of cambium with little left to flow through xylem and phloem. Trees are falling—one about fifty feet away, two others a few hundred feet away. I witness them coming down, their last exhale, a huge *WHOMP* startling the duff beneath my hips. I need to get out of here.

Blaze-orange vests wrapped around guys with guns streak by on quads. A pickup with four guys in camo creeps and crawls over the bouldered two-track road behind me. I crouch lower, nestle myself deeper into position against the tree. But I know I need to get out of here. The wind isn't letting up, and the next tree to come down may make me a casualty.

After the conspicuous hunters pass, I stand, hoist my pack and rifle, and tiptoe my way out toward the pickup. It's midday, time for lunch and a quick nap before heading back out for the evening hunt. I crawl into the back seat, situate the pillow and blanket between piles of gear, and lower myself to my side, knees bent, boots hanging slightly off the seat. I tug my white camo coat over my head to block out light and sound. I'll rest just a little bit more. I'll let them pass, continue their search, drive on while I nap.

I cuddle into the crocheted blanket, loosen my grip. For now.

The elk are napping too.

I hear them calling to each other, penetrating the air with a high, single, round note—intentional. Not a bird. Not a coyote. Something guttural, different. Each individual call is followed by a deep growl. Sounds like hunger.

This part of the bosque is thick with willow, tamarisk, privet, grasses. Not dense with tall canopy trees, more wispy, intermittent. Silty river floodplain. Dusk.

I see the two cats. They're a cross between wild and domestic. One is a milky, dappled blonde with blue water eyes. The other is auburn, reddish. Green eyes pierce. They're both long-legged, lanky.

At first I think they're males on the verge of a fight, the way they pace and stare. But I see that the red one is a female, her vulva so swollen and wet, it drips from her body, bulging between her hind legs from under her vertical tail. They move, one around the other, circling at a safe distance, the growls intensifying, a crescendo of tension.

I have a large stick, a fallen dry limb. I hold it up, show it to the female. She wants me to break off a little piece and place it in front of her face, at the ready. She wants to be able to bite down on it.

As the distance between them closes, I see her genitals in detail, her sex spilling out. Bluish red. Moist. Shiny. Ready. She anticipates the pain to come.

Her teeth clench the dry wood.

❦

HOWLING WIND ROCKS the Tundra, rattling me awake. The snow has let up. The clouds, heavy and dull, loiter low in the valley. Seems like they can't decide whether to stay or go, to lift and lighten or unload more wintry precipitation.

Taking their cue, I settle into the comfort of the cab, heater on and hot Darjeeling tea with cream from the thermos in my cup. I peel the tin foil from the sides of the scrambled egg, pepper jack cheese, and green chile burrito, sink my teeth into the soft sheath and savory protein. My belly growls, taking in one bite after another. As I sit and munch, I watch more guys in trucks go by. In one hour, there are twelve vehicles that pass. "Public land," I mutter with an eye roll.

I figure the trick is to go where they don't, to walk deep into the inconvenient, inaccessible places where the quads and trucks and other hunters can't or won't venture. "Push beyond," I whisper to myself between bites, finishing the burrito and folding the foil into a tidy square.

A heavy Dodge diesel rumbles by, the muffler hanging low, jiggling over the deep ruts and potholes. The dudes inside scan the edges and clearings, eyes penetrating through rolled-up windows. How do they spot the tracks, sniff the sign, listen for the crack of twigs and pine needles beneath startled hooves? How do these guys do it? How do they make the stalk and kill from a driving position? I wonder if they're the clever ones, canvassing the terrain, covering more ground that way than on foot. Maybe the truck is the best tool.

I step outside, push my wool pants to my ankles, bend, and pee, feeling the dull ache of the swollen ovary, then get myself dressed for the evening walk. The sky has lifted. Intermittent blue peeks through and the wind has died down—a sunny invitation to try again, to return to the place of origin from the morning—the dark wood—that maybe isn't so dark now, not so scary.

I head that way, toward the meadow-forest edge where I began in the dark nine hours earlier. Tracing my tracks, I step with more confidence through the snow toward the dense spruce. Turkey tracks catch my eye—was this flock of about five here earlier, or did they pass through as I lunched? I take note of this spot, imagine returning come mid-April for the spring turkey hunt.

I descend into the shadows, the sun lowering himself in the west. I decide to return to the place where the elk congregated in the morning, where the one young cow nearly plowed me over. I figure they'll be coming from the opposite direction now, emerging from their bedding areas and heading toward the grazing grounds of night. If I set up on the edge where there's a clear view up and down the slope, maybe I'll be ready—and steady—enough to make a shot.

But my GPS isn't working, I can't locate myself on the map. I turn it off and on twice, push different program buttons and try to get it to come to. I know where I am and where I want to go for the night, but I recall Patty's words as I left her and Olivia at home, "Be careful. Don't take any unnecessary risks," she admonished.

Is this a risk? I wonder. What can go wrong—getting lost—and what can go right—getting an elk—are both more precarious in the dark. I know finding my way back to the truck with or without an animal on my back can be tricky, disorienting at night with no visible landmarks.

So I choose to turn around and find a clearer opening closer to where I parked. I figure this, too, could be a main route to and from the meadows where the elk will meet up again come nightfall.

As I rotate back, I hear a quad then see the riders, an older man with a young boy, drive past. I stay vertical, pressing my chest into a thick fir trunk, holding steady while they scour the area. I conceal myself, letting them pass, then continue on toward a slope to the east I've never walked, one with a view to two meadows and a drainage below. It's 3:00 p.m., just before prime time. I need to find a spot at the edge, sit, glass, wait—and be ready.

"Walk where you can see you've walked. Go the opposite direction. Play it safe." The day's directives move through me as I resist the temptation to go deeper, farther. "You always want more," a past lover's words sting as accusation.

Commotion to my right yanks me from the daydream. There, in the clearing where I had started the morning's walk, two young elk drift toward me. "What in the hell are you doing? You're going the wrong way. Don't come to me . . ." I tell them as they move toward the ridge rather than heading down to evening grazing grounds.

As if coming full circle back to dawn when I dropped to my knees and propped the rifle on the shooting sticks, I do the same now, anticipating where the elk will be in a few seconds once I'm set up. I kneel, fling off my gloves, position the Mauser and the scope, and dial the magnification down now that the elk are within seventy-five yards.

They sense the danger of me and bolt. I swing left, land the cross-hairs on the kill zone of the second elk, and fire. Slamming another round into the chamber, I stand and take another shot just in case.

The elk reels and tumbles, finally falling about fifty yards from where he was when the bullet first made contact.

❦

REVOLUTION: AN OVERTHROW, transformation, a shift in direction in favor of a new system, a radical change in the established order. To revolt, revolve, evolve.

To undo and be undone.

The Moon circumambulates the earth counterclockwise. Her twenty-eight-day path reveals itself to us earthlings as fractions of darkness and light on the swell of her womb. New, her most concealed self, when the earth obscures the sun's light, to waning gibbous, and finally full, when she undresses, shameless, illuminated by her lover, Sun.

Our galactic relatives and we on Earth move counterclockwise in space, circling each other in orderly agreement, the rules of time and light and distance danced by cosmic choreography. Counterclockwise, contrary to the human hands of time, contrary to control.

Moon. Celestial heroine.

She swims high in the night sky, luring the veil of clouds beneath her to the east.

Who's revolving whom? Who turns the other?

❦

SAFETY ON, RIFLE over my shoulder, I hurry toward the elk with caution in case adrenaline electrifies one last flight-for-life bolt. As I near, I see the breath has stopped, the eyes are still. I crouch down, listen, and look for final flutters. The elk lies motionless.

I see that this elk is a young bull, antlerless, like the first one up on the Vermejo ten years ago and the young Wisconsin buck. Where is the mother of this one who's likely a brother of the two that were just trotting, full of life, through the meadow? Were they hidden in the shadows at daybreak, shielded by the other cows' watchful eyes? Had they bedded down in deadfall as the mothers grazed? How could our paths have intersected like this now? They were going the opposite way too.

Pulling a tarp from my pack, I begin the field dressing with focused intention. Night follows at the arc of the setting sun. Rather than quartering the elk and packing him back in loads, I want to keep him whole. I want to bring him to the house, lay him, centered, between the kitchen and living room. I imagine that his bardo—his time between life and death—can be prolonged and somehow savored rather than hurried to make meat.

Olivia, Patty, family, and friends could come, reach for him, touch his face, stroke his back, smell his home on his hooves. We could cut together, sever hide from muscle, pull the meat that will feed us, listen to the stories he tells.

❦

"OH MY GOD! Congratulations!" Patty and Olivia text back when I let them know there is an elk down. "Do you need anything? Do we need to come help pack him out? What can we do?" Patty asks.

"No, you don't need to come. I don't need help. Please just go outside. Right now. Go out, kneel to the ground, say thank you."

With the little bull wrapped in gauze bags and covered with the tarp in the pickup bed, I drive back to camp. Other hunters have returned, gathered around their campfires, sharing the day's stories. I pull in at the Airstream, turn off the engine, exhale. Looking north to the emergent star dance, I phone Rose in Taos, about sixty miles away.

"Hi, Rose. Do you have a minute? I want to share a story."

MAKING TRACKS

I AM A WOMAN who hunts alone most of the time now.

This way means no one asks why or makes me give reasons for choosing a ridge to climb or a draw to walk. Or questions why I lean into the ponderosa and listen, just listen. This way there is no one around to feed, coddle, explain to, or apologize to. No one yanks me their way or wonders why I go mine.

I carry no one else's weight.

I am. Without reason.

The rule books carry less leverage. Leaning into perfection has loosened. When the days are distilled into life and death moments and attuned to tiny toenail prints in the soil and subtle wind shifts, my old identities pale.

Out here, alone on the hunt for deer, elk, and turkey, I open like the river bending back into her own body as if she changed her mind about which ocean to give herself to. As if she might even defy the Continental Divide and cross over, doing the one thing they told her she couldn't.

An oxbow. An island. An edge. A riverbank cluttered with fallen timber and tangled grass. Here goose tracks make muddy riddles on cobblestone. A heron stands still, wet legs and twenty-one cervical vertebrae curved into an S of neck muscles that strike to zap the fish. The cougar sips and moans at night. Mergansers paddle, dive, float, and lift off.

She does not fit between the lines. The river draws her own map.

A bear walked me through the contours between a mountain saddle above the creek during a fall elk hunt two years ago. I did not see her sloped hips or wet nose. I did not stiffen with fear or seek cover. Her tracks lead the way from high to low following the trees' shady skirts, interspersed with dungs plops as conspicuous heaps of crushed scrub oak acorn shells and rose-blue juniper berries. A twisted piece of green plastic too.

A herd of elk grazed then napped on the north side in remnant snow drifts. Later, when I traced their tracks and piles of poop, when I saw where their heavy warm bellies had pressed the grama onto itself like fine strands of a toddler's tousled hair, their way made no sense. They covered no ground, did not make efficient work of getting from here to there.

Aimless.

The tracks follow each other and make game trails, diagonal lines up slopes or crisscrossed through meadows. Sometimes the tracks disappear. Where did the animals go? How? It's as if they've grown weary of my tracking, sniffing low, glassing high, looking for them.

Maybe they want to be alone, too.

❧

NOW I GIVE in, but this time to myself, to the animals, the river, the wisdom, and ways that are larger than human. Plans on paper confine, restrict. I say yes to the humans less, design less, fashion fewer pretty places that perform and satisfy. Twenty-three years of landscape as profession slip through my hands.

The land, the animals undesign me.

They are beneath my skin now—the river, the tracks, the musk, the rut calls, and sensory meandering. How may I serve the four-legged and winged? How can I shed the burden of cultural skins and revive what was born unto and within me?

❦

WINTRY WIND WHIPS my bangs into my eyes, and powdery soil particles spiral in clouds around us. Grit in our teeth, we smile. I'm here with the stone crew. This will be one of my last landscape installations, one of the last times I implement a design vision on the ground.

We spread the 24 × 36 in. drawings out on my tailgate, weigh the corners down with rocks and hammers. The grade has been set with the skidsteer. There will be an entrance walkway and three landings with steps between the parking area and front door.

It's my job to dream the design, to imagine what can be programmed to be pretty in a place where soil has been scraped, trees tugged from their roots, boulders rolled to nearby gulleys. I imagine alone on paper—doodling, sketching, making shapes of plants and wayfinding routes based on site visits—and have conversations with the owners and construction foreman. I draw future maps.

I listen to them, but mostly I listen to other voices.

Two does and one fawn cross from west to east, browse the tips of fruit tree branches on their way to the river.

Turkey vultures circle on north wind.

Lichen clings to craggy stone facades: neon orange, chartreuse, periwinkle, black, white. How long have they lived here, holding on like this?

Pincushion cacti tuck themselves in nearly flush to the ground. They'll time their tiny, yellow-centered, pink bloom with the show of spring. What pollinator will slow down to see this shy one?

Elk rub cottonwood saplings, scrape bark, reveal tender cambium. I see the dark brown hair from between their antlers stuck on the wounded trees, strands stunted from friction.

Their hooves sink into wet clay, cross the river, and head across red soil to thick cover. Looks like there were at least three.

The client tells me we need to make exclosures to keep them out. To get those trees to take hold. This will be the third time trying.

During these years as a landscape design-build professional, I have worked alongside many men, most of them from Mexico.

"Escuchemos. Las piedras . . . están cantando? Quieren bailar?" I ask the guys. *Let's listen. The stones . . . are they singing? Do they want to dance?*

They stop, hold still, listen. We look at the open pallets of quartzite transported here on two semitrucks, the pieces of thick slab stone laying heavy on compacted, red construction dirt. Leathery-faced men with wide, calloused palms, worn work boots, stained denim, and broad-brimmed hats watch me, shovels and pickaxes at rest beneath their elbows.

I imagine they think me loca. A white woman named Green with blue eyes and yellow hair. Do they wonder why we stop, listen, calibrate to the pace of stone instead of the ticking of Time is Money?

Cosme. Rafael. Miguel. Gilberto. Luis. Orlando Sr. Orlando Jr. Ricardo. Fabian. Jorge. Joaquin. Nathaniel. Eddy. Edith. Fernando. These men, many from the same family, have committed to this project. There are four thousand square feet of stone walkways and steps to be laid for a guest house that's being constructed on an ample ranch about an hour east of Santa Fe, New Mexico. We're starting today, mid-January, with an icy skiff of snow frozen to a crisp crunch by the near-zero temperatures last night. I wear long johns, wool pants, layers of insulating silk, wool, and fleece, a thick beanie, and gloves. I'm dressed in layers that I typically wear during hunts this time of year. Today is cold but not too cold to work. In years past we paused projects for at least three winter months and resumed when the ground thaws. Lately we've been able to make progress all year with consistently warmer temps and soil that hasn't frozen solid.

There are countless pallets of quartzite to work with, but neither the guys nor I have touched or learned the material of this stone; we do not know its weight or depth of its origin. We usually work with locally quarried sandstone, a softer, lighter sedimentary rock that chips and flakes in layers and comes in colors like Colorado red, buff, oak, and buckskin. But this quartzite is different—heavier, substantive, dense. The pieces with rough edges range from three to five feet across and weigh up to four hundred pounds each. With veins like liquid bands of white and red and gold and silver, we remark how each one has its own face, its own feeling.

"Mira, aquí está una mariposa," or "Aquí está Medusa!" or "Esta es plata y oro . . . preciosa." *Look, here is a butterfly . . . Here is Medusa . . . This is silver and gold . . . precious.* The guys slow down, allow themselves to take in the texture and gravity of each stone. I watch their fingers trace the craggy edges, their palms press into the irregular surfaces as if some sort of transmission is taking place from stone to skin, earth to human. This metamorphic rock formed in the folds of mountains under intense heat and compression over long, geologic time tells stories of change beyond what we witness in a human lifetime. Does this stone know that veins in our bodies, too, carry trace minerals of iron and calcium? That we have emerged from the earth as well?

"Quisiera conectar esta casa con la otra allá . . . Podemos poner las piedras en diagonal, como a cuarenta y cinco grados? Entonces hay una conexión visual entre las dos lugares, y están en conversación juntos," I suggest to the crew that we create a visual connection to the main house by orienting the stones and the seams between at a forty-five-degree angle, diagonal from the portal of the primary residence. I envision a visual and sensual connection between this and the other house, a wayfinding through stone where widely spaced outcroppings embedded in a native grass and wildflower meadow merge into a continuous flow, mimicking the Pecos River that runs about seventy-five vertical feet below the house. The walkway will ebb, flow, widen and narrow, inviting people to do the same: emulate the flow of water, feel her subtle and vigorous course, watch how she bends and curls herself along the rocky, willowy banks. What does it feel like to step fluidly rather than march in straight-line surety?

❧

I ARRIVE AT the castle of my new lover. Once inside, I want to go to the heart of the place—the kitchen. Oddly, this kitchen is located in the castle basement. I take the elevator down, down, down, hoping to smell what's cooking as I get closer. But there is no scent and there are no cooking sounds—no pots and pans clanging, broth bubbling or knives chopping at cutting boards. When I arrive and the elevator doors open to the kitchen, there are no cooks, no food. Sterile stainless steel, shiny glass, and an unused, new stove stand, cold.

I see that there is a massive vending machine with multiple options of Lunchables: plastic wrapped fake food with no expiration date.

Then, the lone remnant morsel of real food bounces out from beneath the mattresses where I had been sleeping.

A pea!

Without hesitation, I reach for it and pop it in my mouth.

❧

ON THE MORNING I am heading south to hunt for quail . . . I wake to the sound of heavy breathing and the rustle of clothes—too much commotion for this dark winter dawn before low sun has warmed the bedroom walls. The pea still rolling, dreamy, in my mouth, I hear, "I'm leaving!" The new lover snaps at me as I turn on my side, bend my elbow, and prop my cheek up with my palm.

"It's so early. Why are you going?" I ask.

He turns the doorknob and marches out of the bedroom. Memories slip in from the night before. Sensing some shift, I had tried to soften him. "What's your pleasure?" I asked, slathering lavender oil on after my bath.

"Get on your knees," he responded, cold.

This morning my belly churns, electric with fear and confusion. Sitting up, I pull my bathrobe over my bare shoulders, stand, wrap the fleece fabric around my torso, and loop the belt at my waist. With slippered feet, I pad lightly across the floor toward the door, where he bends over to pull on his boots. Olivia is still sleeping. Edmund and Opal remain curled on the couch.

"Don't you want to stay a bit? We could sit together and have tea? I'll light the fire. Tell me what's wrong," I coddle.

"*No*. I'm leaving." His lips tighten, eyes squint, avoiding contact with mine. He's as cold as the January morning, as dull, gray, and merciless.

"Why? What happened?" I remain soft, open, as if it's up to me to extract, absorb, and heal his irritation.

I watch him tug his boots on, pull the sheepskin coat over his shoulders, tighten his lips. A protest. A tantrum. He wanted to be invited. He wanted to come along. He wanted to be my everything.

He storms out the sliding glass door, picks up the circular saw he had brought over the night before, and stomps to his truck. He thought the crew should use his saw at the jobsite. He insisted that they and I need him.

I tell him, "I'm going quail hunting. Alone. And the guys at the jobsite know that stone in their bones. Your tool is not theirs. Your desire is not my directive." My eyes gaze past him to the east, watch for which way the wind teases the dangling dried crabapples. I'm already halfway to the hunt.

I hear the engine of his truck roar up the road, past the fence and our east window.

I will leave later today with Opal Luscious the only one at my side.

The weight of carrying and caring for others, the constraint of pleasing and serving will subside as the miles click beneath the truck and Airstream as Opal and I head south.

Open skies lead the way.

❦

THE GUYS TRANSPORT the metal-strapped pallets using a skid-steer and set a few of them near the far end of the new construction site where the first set of steps will be formed. As Luis severs the rigid metal bands with tin snips, we all stand back in anticipation of the shifting weight. The liberated stone can easily sway and fall when not bound together.

The nails in the wood of the pallets creak. The massive bodies tilt and settle.

As I remind the guys to take care of their backs and their bodies, as I encourage them to relax into this stone, this project, and the site, I step back, inhale, and consider my own loosening. The design drawings, the digital presentations, the budget spreadsheets, measuring, and calculating are over. The client has said yes. The contractor has agreed to the plan and timeline. We're here now to bring the vision to life.

I run my fingers along the lip of the stones, press my palm onto their backs and bellies. Their surfaces remind me of my own surfaces, smooth and unblemished where protected, then rough, fissured where exposed. I feel multiple textures converge, see tales of time on their faces, too. I crouch down, bending at my knees with my hips low to the ground, "Dígame. Dígame, almas bonitas. Dígame lo que necessito hacer. Dígame donde quieren estar."

I ask the stones to speak their desire to me, to whisper where they'd like to live now, next to whom and with which side up or down. This stone speaks a new language. Maybe I can coax them into making this home now, into allowing us intimate proximity into their world.

The guys and I dance together—cautiously—testing the waters of connection established over time. Even now, after many years and many projects shared, my original tongue and cultural textures are different from theirs. We converge through Spanish with the stone, the soil, and plants as our connective tissue. They help catalyze a growing kinship grounded in the earth, where we may recall our original mother tongue together. Here differences dissipate.

I slow my body, adjust the pace and the ambience to match our surroundings: the Sangre de Cristo Mountains and the Pecos River, red rocks and arroyos shifting with wind and water. Four deer glide on tip toes, ears piqued in our direction. Cougar scat dries where the curve of the ranch road meets the driveway.

This is no ordinary jobsite.

❦

"COME ON, OPAL! Let's go!" She jumps into her kennel in the back seat of the idling Tundra, all wags, and a blur of ecstatic spots. This girl knows we're heading out for her favorite kind of fun. The shotgun and the Airstream are her cues that this trip won't just be our daily walk close to home in the Caja.

I situate the New Mexico Gazetteer between the console and driver's seat, set the water bottles in their holders, fasten my seat belt, and shift into drive. The Airstream tugs at the hitch as we roll out of the driveway and up the gravel road. With the Sangre de Cristo Mountains in the rearview mirror, I anticipate the jagged ridgelines of the Chiricahuas down south where the ibex and desert bighorn sheep scale vertical rock walls and scramble down scree, where lizards pump their chests against shifting sand in sync with the sun's beat.

The drive south toward Rodeo, New Mexico, in the boot heel, is about four hundred miles and will take six or seven hours. Situated at the southwesternmost part of the state, bordering Arizona and Mexico, the desert here is home to snowbirds, northerners seeking sunny refuge from ice and snow, as well as coyotes, jackrabbits, deer, javelina, quail and sun-streaked locals. Tourists and travelers find their way, too. Those whose curiosity is piqued by the lure of the desert, ghost towns, mining ruins, rusty wind-whipped tin, fossils, and mineral gems.

The Madrean Archipelago, with elevations ranging from three thousand to five thousand feet, is also known as the Sky Islands in the United States. The area is a combination of valleys and parallel mountain ranges, called cordilleras, and is similar to the Chihuahuan Desert, but receives precipitation enough to support grasslands and woody vegetation. The extreme, rugged highs of the Animas Mountain Range and the low grassland valley are both barrier and bridge. Passage may be facilitated or obstructed, depending on the type and direction of travel.

Rodeo is thirty miles south of US Interstate Highway 10 and just one mile east of the Arizona border. Mexico lies about fifty-five miles due south. I aim for this general area, knowing I can move between boundaries of both states in search of Gambel, Mearns, and scaled quail; all three species converge here. I position myself for the most flexibility, ease of movement, and ability to trace tracks through different habitats and ecotones. Crossing political boundaries into Arizona is nearly effortless and only requires an additional hunting license as a nonresident. They welcome my tourist and hunting dollars and offer land that's identified as public.

I will steer clear of the border to the south where a shotgun would likely be regarded as anything but a hunting tool.

❧

AT THE JOBSITE, while Cosme cruises the skidsteer loaded with quartzite into place, Jorge reaches across the piece of stone that will establish the height of the first set of steps. He signals Cosme to lift the other edge, positioning the slab at forty-five degrees between the new guest house and the existing guest house across the meadow. They heave the stone with their full weight, look up at me, and smile. I crouch down, adding my own body to the effort of moving the stone. The guys make room for me, adjust their reach to accommodate mine, but I know my "help" most likely holds them back. They know better how to do this particular stone dance.

Less might, more strategy. Let the stone move itself, and give more subtle nudges in the just-right spots.

We dial in a groove, translating the drawing that reflects the client's desire for on-the-ground function and beauty. The majority of our clients are wealthy middle-aged or elderly Anglos that have relocated here from urban centers or midwestern convention. Some have chosen Santa Fe as their retirement home, and others live here intermittently between one or two other homes in destination locales.

A climate of four seasons, expansive mountain views and extreme red rock landscapes, a cosmopolitan art scene, world-famous cuisine, and quiet rhythms attract outsiders. They are our bread and butter, the ones for whom we build soil, harvest water, inspire with native plant and edible species, and try to educate about this xeric land. Some want peonies and lush, broadleaf deciduous trees. Others appreciate this more sparse, subtle plant palette. Some resist existing conditions, others embrace.

The crews of three to five men jump in with their specialty as we progress sequentially through each job from grading and drainage, irrigation infrastructure and hardscape (pathways, patios, pergolas), to planting and connecting irrigation lines and emitters to plants and, finally, spreading compost and mulch in all the beds.

This job will require multiple specialty crews and at least one more year to complete. The quartzite walkways and steps will take about nine months. The three thousand square feet of moss rock terrace and planting bed walls took a five-person crew of six months to complete, each stone hand selected, chiseled and shaped to mold together and form structurally sound retaining walls for the planting beds. The client has prioritized the landscape, devoting upwards of thirty-five dollars per square foot.

❦

OPAL AND I continue south through the cloverleaf maze of Albuquerque, past Socorro, the Bosque del Apache National Wildlife

Refuge, and Truth or Consequences. At Hatch, where world-famous New Mexico green chile is grown, we exit I-25 and head west on Highway 26. Plowed agricultural fields span both sides of the road. Their bare dormant soil looks bored, lifeless without rows of chile, *Capsicum annuum,* that are planted in late spring and harvested in late summer and early fall. Sparky's restaurant in downtown Hatch and import stores with terra-cotta pots, kitschy metal garden figurines, and colorful Mexican blankets animate our ride through town before we drop into rolling sandy hills covered with thorny mesquite. I check the OnX Hunt application on my phone to map out public lands where we can walk for birds.

I barely have Opal's collar buckled and turned on before she's off in a flash. There's good habitat here on this BLM land situated near a sprawling industrial metal warehouse surrounded by acres of solar panels. White stones poke their chalky heads out from beneath dried cow patties. Tracks riddle the spaces between the mesquite mounds, evidence of white-throated woodrats skittering during last night's waning moon. Today a red-tailed hawk glides and circles above. Her eyes catch the slightest motion, talons ready to snatch up darting songbirds or unsuspecting field mice.

Opal's spots blur to bolts of motion between sandy mounds propping up prickly shrubs. My gun at the ready, I don't get one shot off. Two different coveys of quail flush more than fifty yards away, out of range.

Back at the truck an hour later, Opal laps up two bowls of water as I shed the hunting vest, unload the gun, and strip down to a T-shirt and flip-flops. January feels more like September these days.

As we make our way south and west, the Airstream bumps along the interstate asphalt with a heavy rhythm. The lover's words simmer inside. The declarations. The demands.

I recall how, a month earlier, when he had decided to try hunting for himself, he returned from his first day out for elk with an arrowhead. "I took a shot at first light," he said.

"How far away was the elk? What was the visibility? What position were you in?" I ask. We had only practiced at 100 yards, felt it prudent not to take aim at anything beyond 150. My body stiffened at his choice to shoot first thing on opening morning at a group of elk nearly 300 yards away. I cringe, thinking of my rifle in his hands. I had let him borrow the Mauser, because his brother's Weatherby kicked too hard, bruised his shoulder.

"We looked for a couple of hours. Saw some blood. Probably from other hunters."

He holds the arrowhead in his palm, about three and a half inches long, and inch or so wide. The tool is matte white, like limestone, with perfectly chipped edges, a curved center and tapered tail where I imagine it wrapped with sinew at the end of a carved spear. "I found this." He beams.

I don't reach for the arrowhead, don't celebrate his treasure. In the protracted moments between him describing and me listening, I imagine bolting like the antelope across the plains, or darting between juniper trees like the black-tailed jackrabbit. How can I extract myself quickly enough, wiggle away from the entitlement?

"When I found it, I felt my ancestors, the hunter-gatherers, come through me. I felt my connection to them. I think they wanted me to have it."

"Hm. Really?" is all I can muster in response.

The slam of the door the other morning, the inflated words, the claiming. How quickly can I make miles between here and there?

I want to turn off and get on some back roads to scout for quail and a place to camp. I want to liberate myself from him, his grip. It would be ideal to set out on foot from base camp each day to hunt, without any awareness of human habitation or activity—no eyes on me and no need to alter my course because of others. With each mile behind me and more wide open ahead, my gut softens, my mouth opens.

I can breathe here. Opal shows me how.

❦

West of Deming, I'm relieved to head south off the interstate and catch Highway 146 toward Hatchita. On this two-lane road, we slice through drought-stressed plains and sage scrub. The land has been hammered by bovine hooves and mouths with too little moisture and no time to recover. Checkerboard state and BLM lands are open to hunting, but the cover isn't dense or diverse enough. There is no mosaic mix of thick grasses and shrub clusters, no vegetation that looks like quail habitat. Cattle grazing, center-pivot-irrigated cotton and alfalfa, and consecutive years without precipitation denude the soil. Remnant roots hang on beneath the fractured, gaping surface as wind whips dust devils across the pavement.

I see towers jutting up from the desolate expanse. As I look more closely, wondering about the purpose of these structures, I see massive armatures on the tops and sides that look like satellite-sized lights. A motion to the south catches my eye. When I pull over to look through the binoculars, I see a white SUV with green writing: Border Patrol. The vehicle cruises along a barbed wire fence line with chains attached to its bumper dragging oversized tractor tires. This contraption wipes the ground slate clean.

At once, the function of the towers and tires become clear: lights to expose nighttime activity and daily swaths along crossings to erase tracks. Sharp, arced claws of quail, sinuous S curves of snakes, round-toed cougar paws, and cloven javelina hooves, along with other tracks of boots, tennis shoes and flip-flops, are methodically removed each day to show who's set foot here in between patrol rounds.

These officials are hunting and tracking too.

I realize what had appealed as open, accessible camping and hunting on public land is actually a war zone. There would be plenty of eyes on me; all humans scaling this territory are seen as suspect. Who knows what sort of destination or target the Airstream would become, a gleaming solitary shelter in merciless terrain? A woman hunting on her own draws enough attention. Questions and comments like, "Where's your husband?" "I've never seen a woman out here on her own," "Wow. That's pretty cool . . . you hunt on your own!" and "You sure you're OK?" have come up when I encounter men on foot, in vehicles, at gas pumps, and at convenience stores. I engage and listen to others' hunting experiences and knowledge of local terrain and animal behavior swapped as spontaneous stories, followed by cheers of "Good luck!" So far I've benefitted from generous sharing of stories, tips, and expressions of caring concern.

And then I retreat, drive the back way, park where the truck is concealed, and walk where I see few tracks. Camouflage conceals me from the animals—and the humans. Here, where I blur into the margins, I can access the animals and am more able to listen from the inside, determine my own way. I follow Opal's lead and learn how to scan for visual cues and trace terrain as scent signs through the nostrils.

She shows me how to obey other messages, how to believe the body first and most. She and I, partners in new terrain, seek sensory—not obligatory—wayfinding.

❦

"CHRISTIE, WHEN MY daughter was here last weekend, she stood on the entrance steps and said, 'Mom, I can see my grandchildren and their grandchildren running, skipping, and playing along this path. This will last lifetimes.'" Linda, the owner of the ranch, smiles as she recounts her daughter's delight in the walkway and on the steps and landings. Linda stands with me out on the stone as the guys continue setting stone slabs. We watch as the crew tamps the crusher fines base before positioning every piece. Each stone takes a minimum of three guys and a skidsteer to move and about thirty to forty-five minutes to stabilize.

"I want this to last. I want all of it to last, from the siding and roof on the house, to the kitchen countertops, to the walkways and patios," Linda tells me with emotional emphasis. "If I do nothing else in my life, I want to leave a legacy for my kids and the next generations. I want them to continue gathering in this place as a family."

As the guys make progress and settle into the rhythm of the material, we get to know each other by asking about families, favorite restaurants, and weekend pastimes. Six of the guys are either brothers, cousins, or nephews, and the others have been working together for ten or more years. I see similar features in the family members' eyes, gait, thick hands, and wide smiles. They work as a focused team, centered around six-day work weeks and sharing rides to and from jobsites and comfort food lunches cooked on comals they prop on boulders or sawhorses near an electric outlet.

"Christie! Ven con nosotros por lonche. Tienes hambre? Yo tengo carnitas para ti!" The guys call to me from the shade with plenty of food to share. I figure the last thing they want is La Jefa hanging around during their break time, so I utilize the thirty-minute lunch session as time to return phone calls, work on my computer from the portal, or find a discreet place to pee.

As I squat, my belly tightens. Legacy. Generations.

What would it look like to not leave our mark?

My smile and nod in agreement to the folks in charge, my punctual arrival at the job site, and my tidying up trash and dutiful rundown of the day's accomplishments contrast with what courses deeper inside. The stone, water, soil, trees, and deer. The arrowhead. Haven't they been handled enough?

My feet seek liberation from these designed lines, imposed imprint. "Vamos a la playa! Podemes salir ahora y llegamos al sur en veinte horas!"

I'm only half joking with the guys about running away with them to the beach south of the border.

❧

WATER SEEPS ACROSS red ground near a clearing that looks like a ranch pump house with a large round stock tank. Quail and other wildlife often rely on ranch and agricultural sources of water when creeks, lakes, and rivers have run dry. The tank is empty, but the squeaky pump still spurts water from a pipe onto the ground.

The 16 gauge tugs at my right shoulder as I press the tone key on the electronic collar twice, signaling Opal to circle back to me.

I lose sight of Opal again but imagine she's just across the draw ahead. I drop down, rise up the incline and push the command button too late. She's just flushed another covey of about thirty birds too far away for me to make the shot. As I call her back, I'm caught off guard when I hear, "You know you're on private property, don't you?" The last of the quail run toward the man slumped on the four-wheeler. I watch them, wanting to follow, surprised at the man for not going after them himself.

"Don't you want to get those birds?" I ask.

"Nope, no ma'am. I'm not hunting." His stern voice and pursed lips sober me up. Opal pants at my left ankle as I open the lever of the shotgun into a nonfiring, nonthreatening position. I realize this guy means business.

"Get on your OnX and locate yourself. This here is private," he declares.

"Oh, well, OK. Thanks for letting me know. I'll just turn back. Must have gotten too excited following my pup and those birds!" I smile, turn, snap the shotgun closed and head back toward the pickup, trying to shake the encounter.

After three days of hunting, Opal flushing coveys out of range, and seeing quail on private, inaccessible land, I decide to head north, back home. As I load up the Airstream and hitch it to the pickup, five scaled quail skitter across the lane to the east. We decided to stay at Rusty's RV park near Rodeo, a seemingly safe alternative to the wide-open desert. Here we settled into an established campsite with bathroom access and retired couples waving hello on their sunset laps around the park.

"Come on, Ops! Let's go!" Opal jumps into her backseat kennel, turns a couple of circles and curls herself into her bedding.

Just outside of Deming, on a two-lane state highway that runs north-south, I stop at a series of orange cones indicating a road-block. Multiple Border Patrol vehicles and officers stop each trav-eler before waving them on or to the side for further questioning.

"Hey there, how's it going?" I ask the young man who stops me.

"Just fine, ma'am. What brings you here and where are you headed?" his pale blue eyes smile back. I figure he can't be more than twenty-five years old. He barely has facial hair and is loaded with enthusiasm.

"Been hunting quail with my girl. Headed home to Santa Fe now."

"Ah, OK then. Go on ahead. Drive safe," he motions me forward.

Before I accelerate, I decide to ask him about the tire-dragging and the towers with lights. "Say, what are all those Border Patrol guys doing out there every day? I see them dragging tires along fence lines and backroads. Is that what I think?"

"Ma'am, you'd be surprised what goes on out here. More than you would ever care to know about. Yep, you got it, they's doing a sort of huntin' too, you know?"

"They're tracking, right? Looking for people moving through the desert. They're looking to catch illegal immigrants, aren't they? With those lights, too, hm?" I push.

"You got it. We got people trying to cross here day and night. And we catch 'em!" he beams.

He doesn't ask to look inside the Airstream or the ample back seat of the Tundra. He doesn't ask any more of me before nodding his head and motioning me through the checkpoint.

I am allowed to drive on.

Red tail hawks circle above, watching for prey. Turkey vultures hover around a roadside deer carcass, jabbing at ribs that protrude from the severed hide. Billboards punctuate the miles with 2-for-1 and All-U-Can-Eat Buffet ads. Blinking neon flashes gasoline and diesel prices, along with the lure of hot showers, laundry, and souvenirs like rattlesnake purses, turquoise pendants, and quartz crystal charms.

The road here feels like a mobile Las Vegas, where a façade of glitz and gimmick obscure a dark underbelly.

We stop at the same BLM parcel south of Hatch for a midday walk. My blaze orange cap and vest stand out against the monotonous background of winter dormancy. Opal and I walk freely with the shotgun, water, and snacks. We move at a pace of pleasure, adventure. I've let go of the getting. I had hoped to come home with enough quail to cook for friends and put up in the freezer. But following our noses shifts my view. Now we zigzag without aim or rational destination.

Time loosens its grip. I mind the arc of the sun instead, allow the birds, miniature stones and curled, papery seed heads skipping on sand, the lacy triple-toed quail tracks, and spiky mesquite thorns to become my compass as I weave my way through them. They do not require my attention, my approval or permission. We exist, as is, without demands.

As I accelerate up the long incline just west of Bosque del Apache, a text message pings from the pocket of my hunting vest. I stretch to the phone and see a message from the lover. When I swipe the phone awake, expecting to see an apology or at least an inquiry about my time away, I read words that bite. "I release you. You may pursue whatever relationship you choose now."

I. Release. You.

In these words I see his eyes on the elk in the crosshairs of the rifle scope, the arrowhead gripped in his hand, the saw thrust toward me.

I delete the text, sink my foot onto the accelerator, open the windows, and drive hard toward Santa Fe.

Arriving home just before dark, I grab the mail bulging from the box, unhitch the Airstream, and unload the gear and food.

Minutes later, as I throw a simple supper of salad and leftover green chile stew together, Luis calls to check in about the week ahead, how many guys he's planning to have on-site, and what materials he'll pick up.

When I arrive on-site the next morning, the guys greet me with smiles and "Buenos días! Cómo amaneció?" The guys and I would tease and marvel at how close the Spanish verb *amanecer*, to dawn or awaken, is to *nacer*, to be born or to birth, thankful that we had the opportunity to be born anew through sleep and dreams each night. "How were you born last night?" became our wondrous daily question.

We exchange handshakes and stories from the weekend. I ask, "Qué soñó? Qué pasó durante la noche cuando estaba durmiendo?" I want to know what they dreamed of, how they slept, what has refreshed or surprised them during the night.

Standing at the curve of the walkway, where the entry planting beds will greet family and guests, Cosme and I join hands, face-to-face. I want to say, "Bailemos! Las piedras están *cantando*!" I want to laugh and spin each other around to the rhythm of the quartz-ite, in the meander of her flow, her song. I want to dance with Cosme and the guys, with the stone mimicking the Pecos below. Who I am here on this jobsite is inner worlds away from my apologetic, unsure self who kneeled for the check the country squire dropped as a passive insult. Seventeen years later, I'm learning to listen to deeper messengers inside, the dignity and wisdom of the stone, the path of the animals, and rooted connection to this tribe of men who feel more like family than colleagues.

I stand taller, shine more brightly, unabashed, like the stone beneath my feet and the moon who invites a wider gaze.

As I approach the guys to celebrate the progress of the pathway, Opal spins toward the wind, locks her legs in place, straightens her tail, rigid to the sky, and lowers her head.

She's been my sidekick at the ranch every day since we started construction. The guys delight in her enthusiasm, tease her with reflections of the sun picked up by their phones and tools, watch her chase shiny motion across the pathway surface and around boulders. "Mira, está buscando algo! Solamente si se mueven, ella los perseguiría!"

Something moves, she chases, hunting in her bones. Now I witness her locked up on animal scent. Perhaps a lizard lies low or a cottontail curls into herself. Maybe Opal smells where the deer walked last night while browsing on newly planted shrubs.

Down south, the quail burst free when she and I got too close, when we didn't hold still long enough. No matter our training and practice with the electronic command collar, the drills around pointing, coming and retrieving, the rewards for following the collar signals and my words for her to obey, Opal chose her own direction. Coveys of twenty-plus birds upended her resolve.

"Déjala. Déjala. Déjala." I whisper under my breath to myself. Dejar, to leave, let go.

The kin I crave among he, me, and she. An elusive we rests deep in my belly, moves in the invisible, suspended breath between words, in the lows and lilt of amanecer, bailar, y cantar. Miniscule molecules of water slick the surfaces of the quartzite, luring colored veins to life, then slip beneath the slab surface to wet dormant darkness below. Neighboring roots take notice, reaching for hydration.

I turn the collar controller off, sit on the sun-warmed planting bed walls, and rest my boots. The pings of hammers and chisels working the stone edges groove me into a different, relaxed rhythm as observer. Opal wags. The crew works. The Pecos flows. Three guys rev the skidsteer and select another pallet to lift and lug over. I hear snipping of steel bands and the stone's exhalation. She's been bound like this for nearly two years, since the job order was first placed, after heavy machinery extracted her from the bedrock of home. I watch as the guys step back all at once, allowing space for the quartzite to land.

As she creaks through the confines of metal binding and lays herself back on the ground, I imagine severing the chains that drag the tires behind Border Patrol trucks. I see tracks made freely, crossing fence lines and stepping through invisible ownership boundaries, lines the land never agreed to.

Imprints of sharp claws, rounded toe pads, and pointy hooves intersect patterns of shoe soles—tennies, boots, sandals—like tiny tributaries converging into a confluence of currents. Tracks liberate themselves, ripple free, let go.

I feel my thumb clicking the safety off the shotgun, my eye looking through the open site. I aim at the glaring tower lights, my index finger pulling the trigger, returning the desert to darkness.

THE LAST TIME

I FOCUS ON THE saddle between two peaks at 10,600 feet during the first couple of days of the hunt. The intersections among creeks, meadows, and timbers are vital elk habitat.

Developing a strategy based on studying maps offers some comfort that knowing would provide. If I just know enough, I can do enough and therefore be enough: a skillful outdoors person, a successful hunter, a fearless woman. My backpack and pockets are stuffed with gear that's about preparedness, protection, and navigation. The compass, rope, raincoat, matches, knives, and headlamp offer superficial, if not artificial, security. What is true is that I don't know where I'm going, and I don't know what will happen.

The mountain peaks strain my legs and my lungs. I push myself higher, breathe harder, burn more. The maps don't communicate the microterrain of tangled understory and crumbling rock outcroppings, the places my toes catch and that tumble me back toward humility. The maze of spruce and aspen—standing and slashed—are beyond articulation on paper or screen. The shadows they cast distort the appearance of stumps into rumps of animals; their breathy sway and belabored creaking exhale just before first light. These characteristics are incoherent without sensation. They must be experienced rather than read as features on the page.

I see the data map makers have illustrated among the topo lines: roadways, gates, structures, fences, powerlines, property ownership, directional orientation, waterways, and changes in elevation. Maps are dense with detail but can only communicate so much.

Defying the bounds of two-dimensional representation, the land speaks her own truth, shares her secrets like an elusive seductress. Her cleavage, erogenous zones, desires, and vulnerability may be absorbed through proximity. Where she cracks when thirsty or hides wetness in spongy moss under the lip of a stone, where spring forbs emerge like tasty lollipops to tempt browsing deer, and where swallows build mini adobe villages on cliff walls. The discovery of these dynamic attributes requires presence. Lift her flower to your nose, inhale. What do you smell? Move your bare feet across her grassy belly and plunge your tongue into her river. How does she taste? Can we understand this way?

Can her body be mapped as sense rather than science?

❦

ART HAS BEEN my mother's husband since 1989 when both of their previous marriages ended. He entered my life as an accessory to my mom, someone I was glad she had and someone I resisted as a male authority figure. I didn't want another patriarchal tyrant watching my every move. We lived in Alaska, where I was raised. Mom would travel to California on business to the US Geological Survey where both she and Art worked. Once when she returned home to Alaska from a business trip, I noticed a gold nugget pendant with a tiny diamond laced around her neck. "Mom, what's that necklace? I've never seen it," I remember asking her.

"What, this?" she grinned looking down, practically blushing. She moved her hand to the jewel, rubbing it between her fingers.

Born November 9, 1927, in Yonkers, New York, Arthur Grantz wasn't supposed to become a geologist. He chose the unlikely academic and professional tack of studying the earth and remote places, mapping mountains and ocean floors rather than become a clothier in New York City like his father who immigrated from Poland in his teens.

Grantz graduated from the Bronx High School of the Sciences in 1945 and Cornell in 1949. Thereafter, he began his career as a geologist, with his first mapping assignment the west side of Cook Inlet, Alaska.

During the summer field season, Art flew with other crew members to Anchorage, Alaska, hopped a puddle jumper plane across Cook Inlet, and was dropped with backpacks, gear, provisions, and mapping equipment along with the other geologists and the cook. They remained there in the Alaskan bush for the three-month field season.

By measuring sets of points and using a compass, alidade, and theodolite, which measures vertical and horizontal angles, Art walked, notebook in hand, and plotted points on paper that would eventually be connected into topographic lines, translating the language of the six-hundred-mile Alaska Range into maps. He was one of the earliest cartographers in Alaska before it became a state in 1959.

❦

A MAP, WHETHER cast as digital displays from cosmic satellite messengers or shown as analogue representation on paper, speaks a specific yet limited tongue. A distancing occurs when a tool interrupts our direct hand-to-ground connection and then another tool (calculator, computer) is used to synthesize and convey the information.

The tools and materials dilute visceral details.

I work at being good at reading maps, at understanding the scaled distances and land features. Calculating distance and terrain into time is crucial when planning the day's hunt. Are there creeks to cross? How steep is the climb to the saddle? What is the perimeter of the meadow I'll skirt at sunrise?

Many times I've sketched out a plan based on the amount of ground I think I can—and should—cover to have been a good hunter that day, expending enough effort in the name of a "real" pursuit or successful kill.

These plans rarely come true. I may adhere to a planned starting point where I don my pack, sling the rifle over my shoulder, and mark my truck location on the digital map, but almost always the cusp of the first hour curves into the second, and every hour thereafter shifts me into unmappable internal terrain. I follow a different directional calling. Now, after a handful of years hunting on my own for elk, deer, turkey, and quail and traversing places known and new, I begin to let go of the ingrained programming. Similar to the jobsite, listening to the murmuration of the stone, the swirl of river eddies, and the languid lilt of Spanish with the guys, I calibrate by my own body and her knowing of the way, or at least a way that is my own.

This hunt feels different since the catalyst of the Gila jake experience, when I could be curious about the connection he opened, and then the last elk hunt, when I allowed the counterclockwise route to redirect me inwards even more. After I meandered with Opal among zigzagged quail tracks and refused the lover's clutch, this hunt isn't confined to concepts like "success" or "should." This place, Unit 53, is new too.

I think of Art, our last visit together and all the questions I never asked like, "How did you have the confidence to make your own map, to find your own way when it made no sense to others?"

Seven days before the elk hunt, I hugged Art long and slow, saying goodbye after a weekend with him, my mom, our family, and Olivia. "I love you, Art. It's been an honor."

I kissed his cheek and squeezed his bony hand as we all crowded around the front door. At ninety-four, his once six-foot-two frame had curved inward to about five foot nine.

He and Olivia looked into each other's eyes as they embraced.

"I love you so much, Art. Take good care of yourself, OK?" she said.

"Let us know when you're having the next party and we'll be here!" Others chimed in, lightening what felt like a precarious farewell. "Yeah, like for your ninety-fifth!"

I know he's more theirs than mine, but I don't resist hugging him another time. We hold each other, standing in silence. I feel his shoulder blades jutting through his plaid flannel shirt, inhale his scent, that of an elder whose days are measured in the rhythm of a rocking chair, cat naps, and sweet snacks nibbled like tiny delights. He has become childlike, innocent again. His gray-brown eyes twinkle. "Bye, Christie. I love you too. Very much."

Now my organized plan for the day blurs. Instead the seductress whispers my name, tugs at my feet, tickles my nose and neck. She entices me in every direction except the papered route. I am at her mercy here. I want to heed her call to go deeper.

I tuck the maps in the pack, letting my body lead the way.

I move in response to outer clues—tracks, sign, scent—and inner cues that rumble from a source that defies reason. I move toward the elk with raven, coyote, squirrel, piñon jay, and cougar as witnesses.

I see where they have stopped to sip. Their motley mix of padded, hoofed, and scaled tracks add depth and texture to dark mud. The deep depressions look locked in place, their outlines remain stiff in this north-facing shaded canyon.

After first light, sitting on a slope where the freshest elk tracks moved upslope, I choose to walk round the contour to a narrow Forest Service road that hadn't shown up on printed or digital maps. I move slowly, with calculated steps, trying to avoid icy patches that will crunch in the otherwise quiet, still morning. The timbers enclose me, darken and shade my way even though the sun rises, illuminating treetops.

There is elk sign everywhere. Branches are broken, tracks press into soft soil, and piles of droppings dapple the ground. I can tell they've been here. But still, no elk.

As I lift my thighs to take each step and swivel my hips to

accommodate changes in topography and obstacles—a fallen tree, a snow drift, a patch of scree—the weight shifts, the belt and straps of the backpack dig in.

I walk, encumbered.

After looking at the US Geological Survey topo map to place myself, I then compare where I think I am to where the satellite device says I am, about a half mile from a private property boundary.

As I put the map away and continue deeper into the clearing, I cut fresh elk tracks that look like two cows and a calf. I head uphill, follow their toe drags through crunchy snow. The wind whips stray strands of hair at my neck. I hoist the rifle farther up my right shoulder, wondering what will appear next.

As much as the maps ground me, center me in what is supposed to be safe by showing me where I am and how to move between waypoints, what tugs inside is a wondering about letting go and being lost. The pack of gear and redundant map references are all supposed to prepare and protect me, but what can I experience out there in the nowhere?

Do the elk ever get lost?

❦

"TURN WEST!" ART reportedly instructed the captain of the US Coast Guard cutter who was heading them into Russian waters while they mapped the Arctic Ocean floor. He had no authorization or premeditated plan that necessitated crossing into this territory, but he must have known this to be a necessary route for his research into the Chukchi Shelf.

Where did this command come from within Art? Had his previous years breaking through Arctic ice, observing polar bears, and reeling up cables with core samples from the ocean floor inform his seemingly spontaneous call? Would he have been able to identify why he chose to go where he went?

As a New Yorker without much exposure to wild outdoors, Art was a kind of renegade choosing geology, irreverent of his parents' expectations. He came off as sure, both when starting out in the field and as a seasoned scientist leading complex Arctic Ocean explorations.

Was he safe because of the maps and tools at hand? Or was he secure in his corporal relationship to topography? Did getting lost even occur to him?

❦

"MOM, YOU KNOW that knife we found when we were cleaning out the car? The buck knife? Do you think Art would mind if I had it? I wonder if his kids want it. I would really like to have it for my upcoming deer and elk hunts," I muster the nerve to call and ask Mom.

"Well, why don't you ask him . . ." she drifts off as she hands Art the phone.

I speak slowly and loudly, articulating every word as I describe the knife. The line goes quiet. I hear a guttural rumble from his throat.

"Well, that would be just fine," he chirps. "You can have it for life, Christie. It's yours."

"I'll get it wrapped up and sent this afternoon. Should be there in time for your hunt next week, hon," my mom says.

❦

DURING THE AFTERNOON I shed layers of clothing and stuff them in my backpack, then slice an apple, munch a few handfuls of nuts, and resist the urge to curl up for a siesta. Though elk are typically napping in thick shade this time of day, they may be moving and could easily wander within range when least expected.

A few days later, after we left the birthday celebration, my mom had called, weeping.

"Hon, Art just got old. He got so old so fast."

"What do you mean?" I ask.

"After you and Olivia left, he went to the bathroom then walked back down the hallway. Everyone noticed. Even Art's son Eric said, 'He aged in the last 30 minutes!'"

Now, as I finish snacking and sit on a south-facing slope glassing for elk, a text message slips through the remote cyberspace and lands with a perky *ding* on my phone from my pants pocket:

"I'm taking Art to the ER. He's having trouble breathing. Will update later once the doctor gets here."

❧

THREE THOUSAND YEARS ago, Westerners began recording the orientation of themselves to place—both terrestrial and celestial. Many of the early maps centered human habitation among geographic features, depicting—or asserting—people's focal point of themselves within a larger, ungraspable world. Domestic and wild animals drawn out of proportion galloped across continents, mountain ranges were exaggerated to show cultural borders, and newly claimed territories were drawn as exclusive islands, surrounded by sea.

Maps etched on bone, drawn into animal hides, and painted on wide scrolls told stories as much or more than they pinpointed location. They were commissioned by kings and crafted by artists to claim identity and character, to personify place through geographical relationship. The map illustrated who a people were based on where they were.

The astrologer and astronomer Ptolemy made maps in the second century AD, situating numerous towns on a world map. His original aim was to do better horoscopes, but he ended up plotting thousands of locations and creating the system of longitude and latitude, the grid we have overlaid on the earth and to which we have assigned coordinates to find and name where we are.

But the first maps, dating back to 10,000 BC, were recorded on cave walls, clay tablets, and even animal tusks. As some historians have noted, the proportion of these maps may be preposterous, but likely served the intended purpose of mythologizing place and people rather than reducing geography to ownership or tangible fact.

Australian aboriginal songline maps wove liminal worlds between celestial and terrestrial. These maps were transmitted orally, telling the stories of stars, the cosmos, and the night sky as a kind of dot-to-dot connection among significant features on the land. Songline maps featured ceremonial grounds, watering holes, and pivotal points of directional change; they mapped the sacred spiritual realm.

Prehistoric Polynesian seafarers utilized bamboo sticks and cowrie stones, a system called *rebbelib*, to represent the relationship between ocean and islands. The maps also depict ocean currents, swells, and wind patterns. These maps reveal wave patterns and are read by wave pilots, navigators finding their way not by the stars but by the feel of the ocean. When at sea those skilled in this sensory art would close their eyes and listen to the reflection and refraction of waves on hollowed out canoes to determine the direction of land.

Those learning the art of wave piloting were blindfolded and guided to float on the ocean's surface for hours, learning to sense the waves, currents, and swells.

Perhaps the ocean was actually mapping them.

Mark Monmier, author of *How to Lie with Maps*, notes, "one map cannot tell the whole story, and healthy skepticism is essential, because map authors who don't understand or otherwise ignore cartographic principles can commit misleading blunders." He summarizes, "There's always some distortion, some point of view . . . no map entirely tells the truth."

If contemporary maps, wayfinding devices, and satellite imagery represent the ultimate technological advances in navigating, what truths have been lost of sensory mapping on bone, stone, wood, and water?

Where, now, have we positioned ourselves in relationship to the earth, sky, and sea? Are we bio- or logical beings? Can visceral, oral, and mythological maps provide real guidance, or are they of a time that's beyond relevance?

What have we gained by supplanting myth, symbol, and the sacred with the surety of science?

❧

"PACKAGE!" THE UPS delivery driver hollered as he placed the box near the sliding glass door a few days before the hunt. Opal wagged her tail, resisted barking.

Bigger than I imagined, I placed the box on the kitchen counter and tore into it, tugging out wads of newspaper. Reaching in, I expected to extract a folding, three-inch, dark brown, and brass knife. Instead I pulled out a weathered, old leather sheath that held a very large knife, more like a dagger and certainly not pocket sized.

I dropped the heavy knife as if it were red hot. This was not the knife I asked for. I had never seen this knife.

Mom and I exchanged text messages and photos of the knife. My mom said she didn't actually know where this knife came from or where she found it, though she believed Art carried it during his field seasons in Alaska.

"Mom, geez, that thing looks like an antique, an heirloom. Are you sure Art knows it's the one you sent?"

"Well, let me ask him," she muttered as she sorted through clutter on his desk. "Oh, right here, I see. This is the knife you want!" She put her hand on the buck knife and recalled how Olivia and I had discovered it a few months earlier.

The knife rested next to the opened box.

"Hon, Art is happy for you to have both knives. I'll wrap up this other one and get it off to you today," Mom assured me.

I hung up and then unsnapped the knife from the sheath. The leather was nearly worn through where it rubbed against pant legs. Nine rivets held the edges together, and their metal had dulled to nearly the same rust brown as the leather. From butt end to the point, the knife measured eleven inches. The handle was ribbed with precisely wrapped one-eighth-inch strips of leather, now an aged dark brown and the steel bolster extended beyond the width of both the blade and the handle.

When I dug deeper into the origins of this knife, I found that it was an original World War II RH PAL 36 fighting knife. Contracted by the US government during the war, PAL produced thousands of these combat knives. It makes sense that the US Geological Survey would have issued this knife to Art when he began his fieldwork in Alaska, not for fighting, but for a different kind of survival.

I palmed the knife, trying to estimate its weight and touch my fingertip to the edge. It needed sharpening, so I got the whetstone and some olive oil, placed them on a brown paper bag on the kitchen counter, sat down and began sliding the angled edge methodically over the stone.

With each calculated stroke, I wondered how I could earn the teachings of this tool.

❦

I'VE JUST PASSED an icy puddle encircled in thick, frozen mud when I feel my phone vibrate. Bull elk tracks riddle the puddle periphery and understory. Multiple piles of old sign and at least six rubs on spruce trunks tell me this is a wallow, where bulls congregated during the rut earlier this fall.

"Considering moving Art home to hospice. More later."

Hospice. This means a decision has been made about Art's chances of recovering. He will simply be made comfortable as his body lets go little by little each day.

The hunt and my focus on finding elk and making meat for the next year's food supply seem superfluous now, as if the only life or death consideration to be made involves Art and what are likely the last few days of his life ahead.

Shouldn't I drop down out of these mountains, pack up my gear, head home, and catch the next flight out to be with my mom? She needs me now.

But there are three more of the five days left to hunt. I've barely scratched the surface. I know there are elk here, somewhere, and the little bull elk from last year's hunt is almost gone; the freezer is nearly empty.

Dropping down from the wallow, I arrive near the truck in time for lunch and sit in the shade to ice my feet. I wiggle my toes and pump my ankles, then push my soles and arches into the iciest part of the creek, welcoming the numbing frigidity and immediate contact with the water that has carved these drainages. My arches expand against a slick stone, my big toe pushes against the current, riffling what was a quiet lull. The skin of the creek connects to the skin of my feet.

I fantasize about walking barefoot the rest of the hunt. Maybe the pads of my feet, if touching the earth directly, could home in on the elk, could lead me a surer way?

I remove my thick down coat and settle in for a quick meal of rye crackers, cheddar cheese, an apple, almonds, and carrots. While hugging the gray wool sweater to my torso and running my hands up and down its sleeves, "Should I stay, or should I go?" paces through my mind. Mom gave me this sweater, along with the knives. They were all Art's, part of his clothing and gear for field seasons in Alaska. He is with me materially and emotionally.

❦

PRESSING UPHILL IN the dark before sunrise the next day, my resolve asserts itself. My plan is to reach the ridge before sunrise in the hope of intersecting any elk moving north to south.

I've already sweated through my first merino wool undershirt but don't want to take time to strip down to something cooler. I still have about a half mile to the top and the sky is beginning to blush. Daylight will break through the timbers soon. I need to keep moving.

But eventually the land works her way inside me. I pace myself, adjust my rhythm according to the wind and weather, the shifting light and terrain, reminding myself to listen, to navigate by other messengers. I see scat from coyotes and what could be fox. Thick, ropy wads of elk hide eroded by weather and foot traffic show where cougar has been.

This morning the forest, the switchbacks, the meadow below are all quiet. A shy breeze whirs around my exposed earlobes. I notice spruce tips turning pink just as I round the last switchback. I slow down, tiptoe before topping out in case any critters are above, unaware of my approach.

Six hours later, wiped out, I abandon my plans to continue along the property boundary. Something calls me back to the other direction and beyond where I first crisscrossed upslope. I backtrack a few miles then continue east. I'm on the back side of something here, a shadow between known points. This path I forge is my own. I do not follow other human or animal tracks, I don't try to situate myself on the topographic pages. This north side of the ridge feels darker, quieter, a less welcoming edge heightens a different kind of alert in me. The elk could be here, far from roads and hunters.

When I intersect the soft opening of a saddle that I hadn't spotted on the maps, where the trees disperse into thick wads of grass that fold over a creek, I drop in as if switching between thriller and fairytale scenes. The space calls for slowing, sitting, lingered pauses, and deeper listening. I decide I will set up here for an evening watch later. Surely, something will stir in this mythic meadow, a place that feels suspended between here and there. The elk have got to be somewhere close.

Sitting down to rest, I peel off Art's wool sweater, look down at his knife in the sheath at my right hip. It has rubbed flakes of rusty leather onto my green wool pants. I want to use this knife. More truthfully, I want to know how to use this knife.

Did Art butcher caribou with it in Alaska for the crew to eat during the summer? Was it at his hip as practical utility? A weapon of defense?

I also have the buck knife and pull the blade open. I smile when I see that it's dirty, dull. My mom and Art probably used this knife on many beach picnics or kayaking and camping trips. I can see Art slicing thick chunks of sharp cheddar and handing them to my mom. Or pushing the tip into an oyster shell to open the salty, plush wetness and slurp it down. They always kept a beach blanket, binoculars, a backpack, walking shoes, and snacks handy for spontaneous outdoor excursions. My feelings about this knife are as much about Art as they are about him and my mom. Their love clasped in my hand.

The questions I have for Art percolate as I consider the next walk before the evening sit. I'm as much here looking for elk as I am there, with them, holding onto life. I allow our current fondness to sink in. It wasn't always easy between me and Art. As a teenager whose father had recently left, I resisted male dominion. Art and I butted heads about everything. Once when I commented on his driving, he snapped, "Christie, I've been driving longer than you've been alive."

"And you still don't know how." I always bit back.

With Olivia's birth, the distance between us softened. This new life revealed what really mattered.

My life in Alaska began in 1973 as a toddler. We had arrived as a military family with the hope of a new life on this adventurous horizon. Art had been there in the wilds twenty years before, had done fieldwork by small boat, on foot, by horseback, by icebreaker, and he was one of the first people to do fieldwork by helicopter. Walking to and from school, we encountered moose and avoided running into bears. My older brother would hold my hand against winter wind strong enough to move our little booted feet across slick ice. With only about five hours of daylight during the winter, we got used to finding our way in the dark.

Now I want to know more about Art's career making scientific sense of this daunting terrain. His research with USGS, spanning more than fifty years, is internationally renowned and well documented in scientific journals and publications.

"Art was successful at everything he did, you know. Sometimes you wonder if he was just lucky, but probably it was more because he was so capable," Tom Moore, PhD and recently retired geologist at the USGS shares his experiences of Art during a phone conversation a couple of months after Art's passing.

"He was up in Alaska before I was born. I didn't really know the state of topographic mapping in the 1950s but, you know, I think he was actually making the maps," Tom continues.

He goes on to tell me how most mapmakers start from some sort of map that has already been created, or at least aerial photographs as primary references. "Then they'll take that starting point, like an existing topo map or photograph, and work off of that." They're working from something established, something known.

When I tell Tom about the government-issued alidade and theodolite tools Mom and Art shared with me when I visited a few years ago, he's amazed. "Wow, yeah, what you're describing would be like the tools a surveyor would use. A system of triangulation to identify points on the ground based on faraway features, like a mountain top."

Triangulation helps calculate distances between points established on a baseline, a known distance between two of the points. The angles of the triangle are measured with the theodolite to calculate vertical distances, which are the foundation of topographic contours.

This system assumes accuracy of some known feature.

I think about myself following maps, reading visual cues on the land, and trying to match them on the page. Sometimes if I manage to match enough, to verify for myself what I'm seeing outside, I gain confidence. My knowing improves. But the knowing only reveals—and relieves—so much.

The expanse of the unknowns, the places I cannot see or pinpoint, the whereabouts of the elk, and the shift of wind direction are more mysterious map makers. These unknowns require a different kind of reading.

When Art first began mapping in Alaska, I wonder how much he relied on his academic toolkit or if he allowed the web of tundra vegetation, maze of caribou tracks, and grizzly scat to accentuate his triangulations. Could they have been what held the spaces in between points, what made real—and accurate—the dots he penciled on the page?

Tom explains how mapping and geology are done so differently now, "Everything is by satellite, you know. GPS. What we were doing back then was basic geology. We were just trying to understand the earth."

When I ask about Art's specialty, his niche and what he left to the field of geology, Tom pauses. "You know, Art always seemed to be at the pinnacle of his field. He would move from one thing to the next. He did his thesis at Stanford on faults and earthquakes in Alaska, so he became the expert on that. And then, somehow, he learned about geophysics and began mapping the Arctic Ocean floor. He collected some of the original data on the Arctic Ocean back in the 1990s."

Tom describes one of the more extensive projects he worked on with Art, mapping a north-south transect across Alaska, roughly from the southeastern area of Yakutat to the North Slope and Prudhoe Bay, approximately 1,500 horizontal miles. They were mapping the earth's crust, anywhere from 20 to 50 kilometers (12 to 30 miles) thick. They looked at the rocks and considered gravity and magnetics to figure out what was below the surface by walking miles, measuring, observing, and recording. Their proximity to place was an accepted—and required—methodology, a map-making essential.

I try to wrap my head around the horizontal, vertical—and temporal—scales of what Tom shares. What would it feel like for a life's work to take that long to produce? How would it feel to walk those miles and put them to paper? How does that compare to our navigating with devices now?

Tom sighs and says, "You know, some people would ask me what it was like to work with a guy like Art. He had a reputation, a kind of off-putting edge sometimes. But he was a mentor to me and one of the finest mentors I ever had. He came across like a fierce warrior to get his science done."

Tom pauses as if trying to pinpoint a quality in Art that describes something other than the science in him. He reflects, "The guy worked by inspiration. He had some sort of innate understanding and affinity."

❦

THE NEXT DAY ENDS like a quiet exhale. I sit, my back against a naked, fallen tree situated smack in the middle of the meadow I had walked just before lunch. No elk. No other animals. No activity, nothing passing before my eyes or into my ears except another exceptional sunset. The rising moon, waxing silver, swells, audacious, in the burnished sky like a voluptuous vixen, red lipped, alluring. Finally, in near darkness, I stand, look behind me, and walk to the pickup.

I've barely scratched the surface of the hunt and want to keep going. Tonight I toss, turn, and vacillate between waking and dreaming. I fixate on the shoulds and the right way to hunt the next day. I focus on the task and goals as if I can will the elk into existence.

In darkness, I awake with a start. It's time to get up, though the alarm hasn't sounded. I look at the clock and see it's 3:38. I decide to go for it, one last morning of hunting, and then I will return to camp, pack up, and leave, no matter what happens. I know it's unlikely I'll get an elk, especially given the lack of sign, tracks, and actual elk. No one is seeing or hearing them. The hunt so far has been really slow, say other hunters and the game wardens.

As I get dressed, pull on my boots, and take one last sip of tea, I look at text messages that came through during the night.

Mom has sent photos of Art. I had asked to see him as he went from the ER to hospice at home; I wanted to see his face, his eyes, get a sense of where he was in the world of in-between. Was he trying to let go or hold on? The pictures of Art show him elevated slightly in a hospital bed with red sheets and a plaid wool blanket. He looks at ease, without pain, like he's sleeping deeply.

I write to see if he might like to listen to music—Joan Baez or Rachmaninoff, two artists I recall him enjoying when I was first getting to know him. A few messages later include a video of Art listening to the opera *Carmen*. I watch the video over and over, see Art's mouth moving, his facial muscles twitching, his neck arching slightly. Are songlines guiding him beyond earthly confines?

Other images Mom sends show Art reaching both arms toward the sky, his eyes slightly open. Can he touch the stars, suspended here between musical notes? I imagine him dancing with my mother, twirling her around to the tunes, her hem a lilt of joy. His arms have shrunken. The translucent, pale skin of his hands conforms like a delicate veil over rigidly defined bone.

❧

LEAVING CAMP AT 5:03 a.m., my heart races, my foot presses into the gas pedal with antsy urgency. I munch a couple handfuls of almonds and bite into a chalky apple, watery with no flavor. I finish it anyway, knowing I'll need the energy. Just as the pickup thuds, transitioning from asphalt to rough gravel, I notice headlights coming up behind me. Other hunters. The pressure is on.

I don't like to speed when I'm driving the back roads, entering the animals' home. I'll often pull over and let others by. This morning is different. There's an energy in my veins, almost a competitive edge. I want to get there first. The vehicle remains right on my tail. Agitation rises, I grit my teeth. Finally, about seventeen miles in, I pull over to the gate where I'll park and begin walking. The vehicle, a light-colored SUV with two hunters, blazes past me as I back in. "*SLOW DOWN, GODDAMMIT!*" I yell inside the cab, windows closed.

My tantrum has escalated too far. Before I get out to hunt, I say out loud, "Christie, *STOP*. Just *STOP!*" I lean back, close my eyes, breathe, and relax my shoulders. I wait for the letting go of what's been gripped for so long. I acknowledge the not-knowing that calls my bluff. So many maps, devices, and calculations that didn't show me the way to the elk. So much trying to be the solid professional, the good wife, the selfless mother. Finally I step out of the pickup, look at the rosy eastern sky, and notice the wind direction—north-northeast. I don my pack, sling my rifle over my shoulder, and head out. Walking past the gate, I stop myself again.

This day will be for hunting, yes, but also for paying attention. I say to myself, "Hunt like it's your last time." I veer off the path, set my rifle down, and bend to the ground, kissing the cold duff. Tears wet my cheeks, run to the fleece around my neck. Could I convey to Art through the gray wool sweater and knives all that my body senses in each moment? Could I make this morning his to feel?

I walk, trying to emulate the animals, quiet, slow, intentional. If Art were here with me, he would be plotting points and laying topo lines on the ground, situating the theodolite and alidade to triangulate off the far peak to figure the contours here, where the next fifty-feet line would go. I imagine him understanding how to walk this place with the least effort, like the animals do: diagonally, moving along contours.

I touch the knife in the leather sheath, press my left palm into the wool sweater. Are the tears for the shame of my behavior, or are they for Art and all I cannot save? He and Mom are still sleeping. It's only 5:00 a.m. in California. Hopefully I'll be on a plane late tonight or first thing in the morning.

❦

ABOUT TWENTY MINUTES into the walk, I hear:
BAM! BAM!
pause
BAM! BAM!
P. A. U. S. E.
BAM!

Five shots. Must be those two hunters that blazed past me toward gated, private land. Rather than follow my original plan along the dirt road, I veer into forest cover, hoping the shots have driven some of the herd my direction. I slow down, watch the shadows, pay closer attention to the wind. I stop and glass, reminding myself that I'm not seeing everything I think I am with my bare eyes. The binoculars exaggerate shapes, reveal motion.

Still nothing, so I continue to the meadow's edge. Crouching down near a spruce, with dense saplings in front of me, I see the hunters and their vehicle about 350 yards away in the middle of the meadow. I look closer and see two elk laying on the ground. I watch, my heart and breath quickening.

A whiff of elk scent opens my nostrils. I smell her, the closest I've come so far to an actual, live elk during this hunt. The guys are on the other side of the barbed wire fence that delineates private land. I watch some more, noticing how neither of them kneel to the ground to begin the arduous work of opening the elk, field dressing, skinning, and quartering. I see them fidgeting, looking around, as if waiting for something. Then I see them pull straps from the back of their vehicle. Something feels off to me. These guys aren't getting to work like hunters with downed animals do. They're oddly aloof, detached. One hunter raises his binoculars to his eyes and looks in my direction. I freeze, wondering if he's watching me now.

Just then I hear heavy breathing at my neck. I jerk around, look behind me, see nothing. The breath comes again, heavy, and hard.

Still I see nothing. Rattled, I decide to get out of there, push up off my knees, turn and walk away inconspicuously. As I step deeper into the timbers, I choose to look back one more time.

And then she shows herself.

A cow elk appears at fifty yards toward the meadow's edge. She's dragging her left hind leg, pulling herself along, labored, panting with the two whole legs she has left. The front right leg is shot, too. The rear ankle and hoof dangle, bloody. Only a faint tendon holds them to the blasted knee joint.

She looks at me, pulling herself in my direction.

"No! No! No! Not me!" I tell her. "I am the enemy." She keeps coming as thoughts race through me.

I want to kneel at her side, hold her closely, and rock her, take away her pain like I try to do with Olivia when she's sick. I want to wrap a bandana above her knee, stop the bleeding, to place her head in my lap, stroke her wide ears, and look into her eyes. I want to pick her up in my arms, hold the weight of her against my torso, absorb the blood, the wounding, the indignity. I want to take all that she did not deserve and return to her something whole, pure, and good. Something as big and right as she is. I want to save her, save what's wild and innocent.

I begin to inch closer, and then she screams. She wails deep, like a hard, hollow canyon, a grassland grazed barren and cracked open, a mountain mined to the navel, a rainforest denuded.

The meadow freezes.

Conifers shed their needles.

Rabbits plunge deeper in their warrens.

Ravens halt in midair with no more marbles to roll in their throats.

The sky plummets.

Her scream echoes in my throat, yanks my belly.

The elk is wracked.

I stand, suspended between hyperaction and disbelief. The seconds hang heavy, a life before me, this moment of choosing.

Finally she drops, letting go of all her weight. Her breathing fills my lungs, her eyes penetrate, her scream explodes my ear drums. Could we trade places? Could I set her free, give her my two able legs?

Her screams continue.

Dropping to my knees, I yank my gloves off, open the shooting sticks to support the rifle.

With her neck centered in the crosshairs and her eyes centered on mine, I click the safety off, exhale, and pull the trigger.

Finally her head drops.

Silence.

Dark clouds shroud the sun.

The moon tucked beneath the horizon dons a darker veil. She would be new again if only she could.

The elk's rear hoof spasms, her belly heaves.

The hunters are barely visible now. Their vehicle bumper is almost obscured by the timbers. I sink to the ground, try to take on the wailing. I am no match, no relief. I am not big enough.

❦

"THE HOME HEALTHCARE nurse says Art only has a couple more hours. His body is showing signs of shutting down." The words appear on my phone as I butcher. The cutting of meat is slow, methodical. There is no way to hurry this process. I cut for thirteen hours the first day, moving through the backstraps, tenderloins, and one hind quarter.

"I want to see Art, to be with him. But if he needs to go, it's OK. His body knows what to do," I text mom back.

My flight is early the next morning. As I place the meat in the freezer, I see the elk collapse, hear her voice. Was she screaming for mercy? Justice?

I pack my bag, tidy the house, shower, and hop in bed. Midnight. I'll have five hours of sleep before getting up and heading to the airport.

Tonight I do not dream.

❦

AT THE AIRPORT, everything seems so far from the elk. And Art.

As my brother and I drive freeways and cross the bridge toward my mom's house, he fills me in on the last few days, who's been there helping, how Art's body has changed, shrinking into itself.

"It's hard, Christie. It's really hard," Shaun tells me.

"What is?" I ask.

"The dying. It's hard to be around the dying."

Forty-five minutes later, at mom's house, Art lies motionless, covered in red cotton sheets with his arms tucked to his sides, narrow, like stretched rope. His chin slightly arched, his lips part, breath labors in and out.

Mom pops out from the hallway, reaches out to give me a long hug and whispers in my ear, "I'm so glad you're here." Our tears are quiet.

"May I sit with him? Is it OK to hold his hand, to touch him?" I ask.

My palm feels a fragile warmth in Art's hand. I reach up to his white hair, brush his forehead. Does he feel me? Does he know I'm here, or has his sensory landscape shifted toward the tundra, the icy waves of the Arctic? Does he reach in his pocket for his wayfinding tools or is he able to settle into the body wisdom that guides him to the unknown points ahead? Will the transects he mapped look different from here, this altered body of knowledge on this new frontier?

❦

AROUND NINE FIFTEEN, we turn the lights down, set the papers and books aside, gather around Art as Mom leans into his cheek. "His breathing has changed," she whispers. She clutches Art's hand. Lowers her body alongside his, her face pressed into him, skin to skin.

He breathes, we breathe. He stops, we stop.

The full moon rises in the east. It is November 18, 2021.

"There, there. There it is," Mom says. "He's stopped breathing."

EXHALE

EXHALE

EXHALE

Shaun reaches behind Mom, cranks the window open.

"My darling. My Arthur."

We leave Mom with her beloved, go outside, look up to the eclipsed moon, wordless.

❦

AFTER BUTCHERING THE elk at the meadow's edge, I packed both tenderloins and backstraps out on my back. When I arrived at my pickup, on the other side of the dark timbers, a game warden was there to meet me. "Tell me what happened . . . Can you describe what you saw?" he asked. We both knew that catching the poachers was unlikely now, nearly three hours after their shots were fired.

I rub olive oil and shake coarse salt on the finely grained red meat, supple beneath my fingers. I used Art's small brass knife to slice this muscle from her body.

The tenderloin is the psoas muscle that attaches along the lower lumbar part of the spine, behind the hip joint, and reaches to the femur, or thigh bone. It is the only muscle that connects the upper body to the lower body and is crucial for balance and overall mobility. This muscle pulls our legs up when we walk and allows us to curl into ourselves. The psoas tucks our bodies into the contours of a warm womb, pulls our vital organs inward as we dream.

❦

BACK HOME FROM California, I thaw the elk's head. I've set aside the day to peel the skin and hair from her face, cut her ears from bone, open her lips and tongue and pull them from the rigid armature that's held the soft tissue together. Once I have most of the meat scraped from her skull, I will set it to boil in the stock pot.

Using Art's pocketknife and a couple of smaller blades, I begin the cutting. I see that part of her trachea is still attached, extending beyond the base of her jaw. I grasp the slick, ribbed tube, cutting between ridges. When I investigate the hollow inner sphere, I see her voice box, the curved cartilage that expands and contracts to push sound from lungs to throat to mouth to air.

This is where she screamed, where her voice vibrated in my throat.

❦

THE STOVETOP LIGHT illuminates the simmering pot through the night. I crawl into bed after a hot shower. I imagine the elk moving between contour lines of life and death. I drift with her there too. I remember the elk as she was before we met, a calf nursing at her mother's teat and committing the sensory data of the maternal to her internal, biological map. She listens for the gentle reassurance of her mother's voice. She trails alongside other cows in the herd, embedding secret topographies, the wet flow of creeks and wind's shifting scent, into her viscera. She is able to make her own way.

Her body is in my body now as nourishment, matter, wisdom.

I feel Art's knuckles on my fingers, the feather-light weight of his arm in my palm. I want to close my eyes, to leave the tangible world where reason directs choice, where black and white diminish all colors in between. I want to meet her here in the dream. I want to walk with Art, the elk, the soundless sky, and cry of coyote.

As I tuck myself in, I close my eyes and trace my fingers at the bend of my waist, up my hip, following its path down to my thigh. I imagine drawing topo lines here, following the contours, listening for where she wants to go.

The cow elk seduces me, tells me there is no destination, that the passage, the making of the way, is between and beyond terrestrial and celestial. She whispers, "My feet follow the icy creek, my nose presses into warm vanilla ponderosa bark. I lay in the shadows, cupped from behind by worn stone."

Fatigue pulls me under. The scent of sweet leaves on her breath teases me. "Waves of grass fill my belly. The moon shows me a morning path that brother bear has laid. Star sisters sing me north through darkness."

I surrender, the earth at my belly, the moon on my tongue.

NEW

First lunar phase when the moon is situated between the earth and sun.

Balanced, she is both light and dark, wholly visible to herself from the inside out.

DREAM UNDEFINED

A series of thoughts, images, and sensations experienced day and night.

An embodied, cherished ambition, aspiration, or ideal.

The dream is made real.

2022

NEW MOON ELK II

Day One

Friday, November 18, 2022. Odometer reading: 154,030 miles. 2:30 p.m. 38 degrees. No wind. This place and I have gotten to know each other over the past few years. Here, Forest Service Road 125 just south of Cebolla, where I pull the Airstream in to make camp and where I walk the timbers, cross meadows, and follow ridges and drainages, is a place of hide and seek. The elk tease, dreams guide, and my body tunes me in.

It's my third solo for elk, and it's been almost a year to the day since I pulled the trigger on the cow elk who looked me in the eye as she straddled life and death near Cabresto Creek. The maps, binos, day pack, six days' worth of food, jugs of water, and the solar chargers sit tidily in their places. I have planned and prepared. The Mauser is sighted in, a decent two-inch group of three fired out in the Caja on a balmy afternoon assures me we're on target.

I have all that I need. I look like I know what I'm doing now.

At two hours until sunset, I head out, layered up with fleece and wool, driving up the canyon to scout. Tomorrow is opening day, and I haven't been here since spring turkey season. I wonder how Canjilon Creek has eked out new edges, curled the grasses inward to her flow and tumbled cobble loose, exposing new undercurrents?

❦

DURING THE FOUR years since the divorce was final, Al and I had had no contact. No calls, emails, or texts. Our names barely surfaced in conversations with mutual friends. They knew better than to ask or mention, knew there was no explaining. The chasm between us was felt though not understood. We had tried to make sense, to talk, listen, and reason. We quit us and moved on. But the hollow echoed inside, bottomless. A memory with each step, taste, sight. I had been liberated from the weight of trying, but not fully relieved. A longing tugged; a desire burned. Other lovers hadn't satisfied.

The opportunity to see each other surfaced as a surprise one morning in February when he was driving through Santa Fe. We didn't know it, but we had both been down south hunting quail at the same time within miles of each other.

He reached out by email. "I'm here in town. I wanted to let you know. Didn't want you to find out from someone else. I'd like to see you if you're open to it."

I responded. Another choiceless choice. I pulled on a coat, yanked my boots up, and whistled Opal into the pickup. "Meet you at the first pullout after the cattle guard," I wrote back. We both knew the place well, where we had walked before, sighted in the rifles, prepared for upcoming hunts. We came together in the Caja just thirty minutes after I received his message.

When I hopped out of the pickup, holding back both tears and smiles, his new dog Ellie, a German shorthaired pointer, and Opal circled and sniffed, tentative and curious. Al and I approached with caution too. Our eyes locked, recognizing all that was familiar, devouring all that looked new. His stained Dickie jeans, navy blue down vest with a hole that had been hand-stitched to tuck in the stuffing, black frame glasses, and patinaed leather belt cinched at his slim waist confirmed his identity. This was Al, yes, but some-how, someone different looked back at me. I wondered how I looked to him, "Like a million bucks," he said. But whatever I radi-ated now was richer than any thick stack of dollars.

Who had changed?

Our bodies collided, Al's bearded mouth at my neck, inhaling, my arms circling his shoulders, the rough wool of his sweater against my cheek. I remembered his six foot three against my five foot eight. Pressing into each other, we rocked back and forth, suspended, weightless. We let go, hugged again, let go, a push-pull of give and take, surrendering and armoring. Everything, all at once.

Walking with no direction, like the dogs, we filled time with stories from the vacant years in between. How could coming together be so easy, effortless? Had there really been a rift? Was feeling good again masking wounds or hinting at future meaning?

As we made tracks through the skiff of snow, tips of fingers reached out, touched. His palm pressed into the small of my back as we walked side by side. "I'm so sorry. I've missed you so much. I never imagined we'd see each other again," both of us saying the same thing, leaning in. Our words toppled on each other's like a mosaic of tracks in the sweet, shady spots where straight-line sensibilities vanish.

But we know better than to hold on this time. The in-between, the not knowing, is enough.

❦

AS I HEAD up the drainage, a text from Al dings on the phone to remind me that I'm not on the ground yet, that I'm still in between town and terrain, animal and human, out there and in here. He's at home in North Dakota hunting pheasant, grouse, and partridge, walking the sloughs and prairie. I'm here, 1,200 miles south, walking my own way.

"Walk. Look. Listen. Stay ready," he reminds, assures. We've meandered back toward each other and found new common ground, though we resist labels and categories. Friends. Lovers. Husband. Wife. Exes. Unable and unwilling to name our relationship, we adjust to this new configuration grounded in mutual freedom. We come together when and how we choose.

The elk was not the only one who surrendered at meadow's edge. An old me was left behind, too, offered up to the turkey vultures and the lone golden eagle who shed her feather when I stumbled toward the center of the grassy expanse that day. Spent, with bloody hands and quivering quads after packing out the first load of her body, I had looked to the sky for answers. But the broad daylight of midmorning hid the moon, the grand *She* I had turned to more as time and topo lines lost their grip on me.

Asking the moon "why?" when Al and I split and when the elk cried for mercy, insisting the moon show herself and reveal all that remained concealed in darkness was like hollering into an empty canyon, "Hello, hello, hello . . . Is anybody there?" The only voice calling back was mine, the only reflection, my own. In the moonless meadow I chose the golden eagle feather, my consolation a quill with which to author new stories and new questions I yielded to as unanswerable.

Lost wasn't so scary anymore.

The elk, her blood, tendons, and fascia beneath my fingernails, the pericardium of her heart staining my skin, her scent in my hair, had embodied the ultimate surrender. She showed me how to let go, like the moon on the other side of the earth, invisible yet still powerful, palpable.

Could I trust my own darkest depths now, too, the tidal pull, inward, toward myself?

"Stay ready," I murmur Al's words under my breath, pulling the shotgun over my shoulder and setting out, loosely looking for grouse while scouting for elk. I know that this, an hour and a half before sunset, is prime time, that the elk should be moving from high to low. We could cross paths anywhere, anytime.

As I drop into the Aspen drainage where the lone cow elk had turned and faced me head on four years ago, where I chose not to take a shot because of the off angle, the waning daylight, and my inexperience, I notice their tracks. They've been here and riddled the road with droppings and traced trails through snow drifts.

Long toe drags show a relaxed saunter. A motley maze of tracks on tracks reveal where two or three cows and a calf hunkered together under the fir canopy. They moved and lingered, followed the rhythms of sun and moon, paused mid-orbit to rest. I can practically smell them, but not quite.

Their presence feels more like a whisper, dissipated, barely audible in the west wind. "They *were* here. But now they're gone," I say out loud just as two grouse flush from spruce branches about thirty yards ahead. Startled, I miss the opportunity to take aim as they fly off.

The elk have slipped between my fingers, like ghosts, ungraspable. I acknowledge out loud, "I'm at least two days late."

Days Two and Three

I am walking naked. Glancing back over my left shoulder, I see the newly formed hair growing on my hips and ass. Craning my head back farther for a better view, I hold my breath, look closely at the layer of fine fur coming in. I hold still. Questions paralyze me from the inside: What will they think? How quickly can I shave this off?

Then I look forward, exhale, and say out loud, "Hm . . . ah well," and walk on. I allow the hide to grow in, wild, thick.

The 3:30 a.m. alarm startles me awake, reminds me that it's time for tea and the day's preparation. I touch my ass to determine if there really is fur growing there, then rise from the heavy blankets, disappointed to feel my smooth, human skin instead. I take a cursory glance at the maps, load my pack with a lunch of seeded crackers, thick slices of sharp cheddar, leftover pheasant breast, an apple, cashews, dried cranberries, and chocolate. I lace up my boots and warm the pickup, the heater on high. The logbook sits on the front seat, the pages I had reserved to record this hunt rest, blank. The readiness in me dissolves.

The scream from last year's elk, her collapse and plea ask deeper questions than mileage, weather, wind direction, and data can answer. Angel of mercy. Steward of death. The Mauser. Me. The knowing implied by labels and either-or categories clamp down, fixate, limit. Defying the planned route, questions liberate, aspire toward expansion. Seeds soften with water, burst with fire, receptive, fertile—alive.

The elk's tanned hide, clean skull, and scraped bones once lay at my feet in the house after the hunt. The armature of her rested, centered in my office for a year. I bent to kiss her forehead after pushing the curtains open each morning, situated her sacrum, pelvis, vertebrae, scapula, and legs just so. Her shattered rear left leg, where the bullet blasted clean through, rested in four expanded, jagged fragments but is suspended now, with her other bones, from the portal beams outside. The time had come for her to be beyond four walls, open to the sky.

Dangling ribs and scapula tinkle like wind chimes in evening breeze, dancing with honeysuckle scent. Musical tones hollow and deepen as her marrow dries, insects excavate and suck her nutrient-dense core. Sun bleaches her bones, shines through the thin, mini-moon basins where her femoral ball joint rotated in sync with her hip, propelling her through the topography of home. Her frame casts mysterious shadows against stucco in moonlight, blurred shapes like secrets whispered from the outside in. When I walk up the stone steps near the peach tree and stroke the elk, my hands on her hooves, I wonder about the space she fills. She is at once a kind of daily presence in our home, her body a physiological marvel, and a larger, ethereal myth. I know she is more than the meat that feeds us.

I carried her as sacrifice, her life shepherded from suffering, but what I'm learning is that it is she who carries me each day. Her body reminds me of what is not mine, what cannot be controlled or understood. By night she hovers above me, intimate, in my bedroom. She absorbs my fear—"How many times have I been inches or seconds from death, from something taking my life, and not known it?"—as I extend my hand skyward, reach for her brow, her open eyes, her long lashes. The gaze we hold softens, allows. Her muzzle rests in my palm, whiskers tickle my fingers. She pivots my question, tipping its underbelly skyward, loosening my grip, "How many times have I been inches and seconds from something that saved my life and not known it?"

What is the difference?

I'm in their home now, with her elk relatives, as visitor, observer. A different drainage, but within similar kinship territory. Elk cover ground, traverse fragmenting fences and roads. The question, "What am I doing here?" circulates through me, tempering the adrenaline that typically fuels my morning drive to the hunting grounds. Happy, holistic, holy. Hunters categorized by motivation, as if there are only three plausible incentives.

❦

IN 2018 RESEARCHERS uncovered a site in Peru with remains of a woman and her hunting toolkit, including projectile points, scrapers, and knives, further substantiating evidence from a similar previous discovery in Colorado in 1963. A synthesis of ethnographies and historical and prehistorical data recently released by the Public Library of Science (PLOS), confirms that women were hunters, integral to cultures where hunting was a necessary means for survival. The study, aiming to determine if women hunted incidentally or deliberately, concludes that "in fifty of the sixty-three societies they studied, 87 percent of the behavior was deliberate . . . women took an active role 100 percent of the time." Big game hunting was, as the researchers confirmed, gender-neutral 14,000 to 8,000 years ago. Furthermore, biological anthropologist Dr. Cara Wall-Scheffler noted about the female hunters, "They have different strategies, but they're always going out."

The research cohort found that women were flexible in their hunting methods, adapting with age according to who accompanied them, how many children or grandchildren they had, and what weapons they chose to use. The PLOS report notes, "In one bow and arrow culture, for example, a grandmother was prized for having the best aim."

❧

ON THIS HUNT, my aim blurs into other edges. My mind rests, like the logbook, unwritten. I eat what I want when I want, taking my fill in the morning or midafternoon. I don't cook back at camp after dark. I take handfuls of salty sweet trail mix or bite directly into the stick of salami. I cave into cravings.

Rather than covering ground from sunup to sundown, glassing through the tangled dark wood and scouring the drainages and meadows, as if obeying an oppressive "they" breath at my neck, I pass time, conspicuous, lying on my side, dozing. I dip between dreams and daylight.

Family groups of antelope—does and calves—are sprinkled across the llano, their lips pressing into sparse tufts of straw-colored grama. They puncture the snow cap with dainty pointed hooves, their thin legs like ballerinas on a white-washed stage.

The sun on snow blurs their drifting outlines, diminishes the distinction between above and below, levity and gravity. They look like they could leap once and for all into the bald blue sky, into a place at last without constraint.

I look to the north and see a figure moving up and down the fence line as if stumped by its obstructive presence. An antelope buck paces inside the barbed wire, his gaze fixed on the small herd to the south. The other bucks meander, heads up scanning the horizon for predators, or heads down tugging grass strands from the frozen ground.

He runs back and forth and back and forth like a frenzied zipper that won't open. There's no way out, no way for this young male to reach the other side, to accompany his kin.

My fencing pliers are tucked into the door pocket beside me. I imagine stopping, cutting the four strands between each fence post along every mile of the state highway and beyond. I imagine the cutting, a brazen act of opening, liberating, and reconnecting the creatures that roam with a roamable expanse.

I could unbind, undefine the prairie, unlock the animals inside. My fingers, tugging my own zipper, opening the swollen wetness, the hungry muscles, the taut nipples straining for full exposure.

I want to be extracted from the too-tight should-suit.

With my wide shoulders and able arms, what if I could unply, unzip, unlock myself, shed the skins that no longer fit?

I imagine my hands on the men's tools—a teasing twist. If I cut the wire, I can slip through to the other side too.

Just as I reach to clip the fence, I startle awake. A broken branch under my elbow pokes me to shift into a sitting position. Four hours have passed. I'm in the shady shadows now. I don't jump up or get going. I sit still. Listen, consider endless options.

I could go anywhere, like they do.

❦

THE FREEZER IS still full with the Cabresto elk. Tidy white packages tucked into neat rectangles, secured with a strip of tape, and labeled in black Sharpie are stacked in neat rows on two shelves among pheasant, deer, and turkey. I eat alone now, cooking for myself since Olivia has left for college 5,400 miles away in Barcelona. I adapt to new, solo terrain.

What I want and what's conditioned conflict. Al's "Keep at it. They're there," along with my brother and other friends who text from town at night tell me, "Get up high. Go where they'll be after the other hunters have pushed them around," "Stick with it," and "You got this," fall flat.

When I choose to posthole through two feet of snow on the north-facing slopes at 10,200 feet, the peak of Canjilon Mountain beckons. My knees and quadriceps pump me higher, farther, but now there is no goal, no summit. My body seeks her own pleasure between sun and moon, high and low, night and day.

She whispers of dreams to come.

Day Four

I wake before the alarm at 2:40 a.m. The dream persists, branding in my mind's eye the words *The Faraway Hunting Place*. No image or plot, just this written directive. I decide on Cunningham Canyon, the furthest destination of the three I considered as I laid down the night before, vaguely planning the next day's course.

The canyon, a good hour or more from camp, is unreasonable, far, and now less familiar. I haven't hunted there since the rainy morning alone, severed from Al who sunk into himself back at camp that day. Cunningham, where Olivia danced the bull and cow to me before daylight, where I and the Mauser took aim. I tried.

Four years later, Cunningham calls.

Rather than head up the Forest Service road along Canjilon Creek, I turn west then north, accelerating on the paved highway toward Tierra Amarilla. Speed at this early hour invades, penetrates the dark stillness. Ranch house porch lights glow, silent. A cottontail darts to highway's edge, shows her reflective red orb of an eye, reconsiders, bolts back and zigzags into brushy oak and sumac. My headlights reflect in a lone coyote's stare. She invites me to slow down, watch her cross. Is she heading to the hunting grounds, too?

About forty-five minutes later, just over the Brazos Cliffs that drop down to Hopewell Lake, a young bull elk stands, centered between double yellow lines. I see his blonde rump and the silhouette of his antlers like a moon-laced mirage. Was he stopped in his tracks, like me, by the vision ahead? Slung low, at earth's edge, the moon's underside feigns levity. A hint of sunlight reveals the slightest sliver there like a coy smile. The bull and I stop, trancelike. The almost-new moon lures, "Come hither . . ."

❦

I TURN SOUTH onto the narrow Forest Service road, rattle across the cattle guard, shift into park then step out to pee. At seven degrees, the air pierces my nostrils and throat even without wind to sharpen the bite. Constellations dazzle the blue-black sky. This morning is magic.

Just as I turn onto the side cut that leads to Cunningham, a ding indicating a text from Olivia perks me up. She's eight hours ahead in Barcelona, well into her day at school. "Hi mom. I'm thinking of you out there. Good luck today. Love you." Our hug goodbye a month earlier feels like a bruise, still tender to the slightest touch. We had embraced on the curb as the Barcelona taxi idled and the driver hoisted my bags into the trunk.

We both held on, our tears merging on each other's cheeks. Her hands pulled me closer as she fondled the ends of my hair, sniffed my clothes, holding us forever within reach. As the minutes passed, other cabs swerved around ours while the driver sat, parked, wordless. He knew this parting could not be rushed.

I text her back, "Sweetie, I'm heading into the Elk Dance canyon, remember? The one from a few years ago, that morning in the rain." She has since grown her twelve-year-old body into a young woman. Her dance is different now. She rocks and rolls more, taps and twinkles less.

I silence the phone, tighten the straps of my pack against my shoulders, and press the 168-grain rifle cartridges into the magazine—one, two, three, four, five—then squeeze it into the Mauser and push one cartridge into the chamber. Fully loaded, safety on, I lock the pickup and head past the meadow to the contour where I'll ascend above the canyon.

Time has ticked on. More trees have been felled in this logging area. Elk have nibbled the cambium of aspen slash. I see gnaw marks in white bark, even in the relative darkness. A few hundred yards in, I pause, hold still, and listen where the lone elk had crossed, peed, and moved on while Al and I lunched at the tail-gate.

The then of he and I rushes toward the solo me of now. But there is no hurry. I take my time, welcoming dawn slowly, step by step, to the subtle *putt, putt, putt* of turkey hens. Fresh turkey tracks show me where they've just landed from their ponderosa roosts. As the sun rises, I see the faded green J-shaped sign of gobbler poop and pine needles scratched into piles. The turkeys like it here.

I catch a glimpse of motion ahead. A lone hen skitters down the slope where I had set up on the two elk that morning, shooting sticks shaking beneath my rifle. The calm of today settles that memory of the miss, the not good enough, the mistake I thought was me. The Mauser feels lighter. I grip less. I choose to sit, eyeing the turkeys like a camouflaged voyeur. It's fall turkey season, and I have company arriving for Thanksgiving in three days.

But even if I had the shotgun, my sight would not be set on these birds. They are not mine to have.

❦

FAINT RUMBLES FROM the loggers arriving at work and heavy equipment firing up one canyon over remind me I'm not alone. The echo of a truck up on the ridge drifts down, heading my way.

Rather than reveal myself and make small talk or ask if the other hunters are having any luck, I hide, crouched down and con-cealed behind a mossy boulder. I watch them, a couple of guys in camo, mosey down the two-track, stop, glass, creep along some more, glass and then drive away.

From behind the mass of stony shelter I wonder if this is how the elk watch me, if I smell as offensive and out of place as the thick truck diesel clinging to morning air. Do the elk notice when I drift toward dreams, veer away from the topo lines of the map? Do they make their getaway as I look skyward? Or are they there in the shadows choosing when to reveal themselves, to come into view, into full sun?

Stepping out from hiding, I see the hens have pecked their way farther. I spy them through the binoculars heading up the canyon, where the cow and bull had fled, escaping me. There's a saddle, a crossing between peaks where the elk could be moving now, a perfect place to set up, be ready. I know this hunt requires more than just showing up. There is no blind, no corn feeder, no predictable coming and going. In their home, on their terms, I reposition myself proportionately, take up less space, muffle my motion.

❦

I HADN'T CALLED the biologist or gotten any helicopter survey reports, hadn't even asked other hunters how they'd been doing. Perhaps having done my homework would have shifted this hunt toward *success*, toward a filled tag, bloody hands, and more meat to cut. But those are old terms from an expired how-to handbook that someone else wrote. My new quill snakes colored ink, blurring horizontal and vertical topographies, shedding old skins of rigid, straight, black and white lines.

As I move nearer the saddle, looking for a place to sit with a tree at my back, I imagine seeing the elk, a small herd grazing through the slice of meadow, a connective curve between the mountainous mounds. My rifle at the ready, would I make a move swiftly enough, click the safety off and fire, clean and direct to the kill zone? Do I know how to make that shot now, even offhand, without sitting or lying down, without the support of sticks? I think of Olivia, coming through to me on the phone in this new, long-distance mothering.

I recall the hunt many years ago with Al, when the elk appeared from thin air, the one he never saw, the one I tried to take on my own when I knew enough to lean on him a little longer.

Once she was down I brushed my hand across her exposed belly and four soft pink nipples. Breathing in, I took my knife in hand and penetrated her thick hide at the sternum, heading toward the anus, as my two fingers carefully separated hide from innards.

Spews of warm, gut-scented air emanated from inside. When I reached her udder, the knife pierced swollen mammary glands. Watery milk drained onto my hands, mixed with the blood.

She was lactating. I hadn't seen a calf, or any indication from the cow that she was protecting a calf or keeping track of its whereabouts.

Whose mother had I taken? What calf would be left to survive on her own? Rather than hurry the cut or move to another area, I took the udder in my hands, letting Al continue with his cutting. I inched my nose closer to the milk, smelling the sweet scent. I felt the dense, lumpy texture of her udder and was reminded of my mammogram reading not two weeks earlier: I saw in her flesh what I saw in the X-ray films of myself—tissue, veins, vessels, glands, nipples—architecture of life-giving nourishment. The mother of me in the mother of this elk, Olivia's instinctual hunger at my nipple, and the calf seeking the milk of her mother too.

Something of our similar biology centered an accepting resolve inside me. Had I ever been as good as this elk? Had I ever been as strong, capable? Did I know how to move through my own habitat and fend for myself and my young? Could I see the perfect animal in me through her, from the inside out?

Had I severed this elk's connection to her calf with my shot? I imagined her, the young one, by necessity evolving too quickly into an independent animal, senses heightened, adrenaline activated, at the ready to flee and to run for cover. Now she must seek the safety of shelter on her own.

❧

I FIND THE tree, a ponderosa with a forked trunk, shrug off my pack, and set the rifle down. Sitting on gobbler poop, I loop the binocular strap off my neck and pull the blaze-orange wool hat over my eyes.

Lazy with the heat of the rising sun, I lay my back onto the melting soil, belly up, arms wide, exposed. My body recalls the corn harvest and the dream of Olivia's conception nineteen years earlier when I awoke with, *I'm PREGNANT*, shattering the darkness. The bull's blood mud, soil bound by the substance of life, a floor inseparable from the earth beneath the house in El Guique, this choice made me.

I was thirty-three then, coming into my peak estrus, my body irreverent, unsatiated. Did I have to ask permission then? Do I now?

My hair cascades, uncombed down my back. I line my eyes, gloss my lips, stride across open ground. At fifty-two my desire still runs deep like the cow elk who circle up around the self-proclaimed dominant bull during the rut. The cows gather to form the harem. He bugles and snorts, stomps, and squeals, running at the vagrant cows to stay within reach, within his domain. He demands they corroborate his claim to genetic superiority.

But when I watch the big bull, the satellite wannabes, and spike bull juniors, when I see the mule deer bucks saunter in from the sidelines for a taste of the action, I notice the cows, aloof, wandering beyond the prescribed frontier of obligatory fornication. The cows go their own way.

They wait until they're ready. They come hither when they choose. They stand, rooted, legs spread open while at their peak per their own bodies' governance. The cow elk summons the bull.

She allows him.

Olivia nursed at my breast at 6:38 a.m. on Friday, January 7, 2005, after a "textbook" six-hour labor. Gulping my milk, she had taken to my body, latched on effortlessly, as if she'd always known this familiar terrain of home.

Nearly nineteen years later she makes her own way as a young woman an ocean beyond my body, my womb where she sowed herself as one perfect miracle, defying the 25 percent possibility that the egg of her would be fertilized, the 30 percent rarity of conception maturing to birth, the "impossible" of her father's sterility.

Olivia defies reason, time, and space.

She dazzles.

Now Olivia takes flight, casts playful light and mysterious shadows, creates her own paths, navigates by her own bodily compass. She makes her way.

❧

EIGHT HOURS AFTER waking, heeding the call to the liminal faraway place, my eyelids droop, heavy. The other hunters have passed. The turkeys are surely atop the ridge and, by now, have dropped into the canyon even farther from reach. I no longer hear their *putt, putt, putt.* Noon nears, heat rises. I set the Mauser on ponderosa duff, strip down to my Merino undershirt.

Bunching my jacket and Art's wool sweater into a pillow, I lie down, pine needles tickling my waistline. But today my body chooses her own company. The trying, the pleasing, the killing and packing, the butchering, and the feeding rest too. I have pushed them all hard enough, long enough. The animals tease me, come closer as I let down my guard, disarm my weapon.

It's just me here, as is, Christie. Nell. Green. A simple name and, as my parents said, "not really inspired by anything in particular. Guess we just liked it." I had wanted to go beyond, to be more than nothing in particular.

The seeds, the animals, the soil, blood, bone, and water cracked open a conduit to and through me. They became my home, my belonging. I wondered if, through them, through the food I made, harvested, and hunted, I, too, could catalyze kinship, belonging, reverence?

In the *Power of Myth* conversation between Bill Moyers and Joseph Campbell, Campbell asserts the first storytellers' ancient myths were "a means to put the mind in accord with the body and in accord with the way nature dictates." Campbell emphasizes how "myths are there to help us accept nature's way."

Could this acceptance of nature's way, including the paradox of killing, facilitate a liberating acceptance of my way, the animal way? Are there other females who personify the paradox, the myth that catalyzes connection? Did the ancient female hunters transmit the animals into and through their grandchildren? As food? As story?

Now others send snapshots of iconic sculptures from international museums, images of Diana surface on my phone screen with "Thought of you" captions from friends and family. The myth of this goddess transcends centuries, cultures, shifting interpretations. She persists, vivid, as carrier of messages from the animal kingdom, a storyteller bridging worlds and epochs.

Diana, goddess of the forest and of the hunt, deliverer and protector of life. The roots of her name, *dius*, godlike, and *dies*, related to the shine of the moon. She is also known as Diana Lucifera, "light-bearer." The philosopher Balbus noted how Diana was also called Omnivaga, "wandering everywhere," because she was thought to be one of seven planets and the one who turns darkness to light.

Her identity evolved through the centuries, first recognized as the goddess of the hunt and the wild, then as the deity of the tame countryside. Later she was culturally anointed as a triple goddess—Diana as Huntress, as Moon, and as the Underworld.

As her inner identity changed, so did her outer appearance. Known to wear elaborate robes of gold, purple boots, jeweled buckles, and ribbons in her long hair, she appears as feral, regaled royalty. She is also depicted as keeper of the rural countryside, with toned down, less flamboyant fashion and crowns of innocent flowers adorning her, signaling her as slightly less wild.

Cultural maps employ the three-way crossroads as Diana's mark as a triple goddess. Since she is considered the keeper of roadways, gateways, and junctures, the ascribed symbol is interpreted by historian C. M. Green to "symbolize the crossroads hunters encounter in the forest lit only by the full moon, when they make choices 'in the dark,' without the light of guidance."

The ancient ones, the goddesses, draw their bows, launch their arrows, tease me between the solidity of the earth beneath my spine and the sky above. My name, Green, so simple. The color of life. My worn boots with cracked leather and frayed laces, motley outfit of wool pants threadbare at the seat, layers of fleece and down, and matted hair stuffed into my camo cap serve as practical uniform. Bolstered by sheathed knives at my hip, the rifle slung over my shoulder, and binoculars and rangefinders, all are essential tools in my pack.

A tight skirt, polished, knee-high leather boots, a silk blouse, wide belt cinching my waist, makeup, perfume, sheer lingerie. I wonder if I look—and live—the part? Hunter. Mother. Landscape Architect. Wife. Ex. Friend. Lover. Woman.

Did Diana conform to the identities they assigned, or did she consider them preposterous? Did she come to the crossroads and choose, or did she make—map—the crossroads? Did they map her?

"Who you are shapes the questions you ask," states Dr. Wall-Scheffler. "It shapes the expectations of what you see."

I lie still beneath the ponderosa, seeing the image of the Peruvian huntress at final rest in her sleep burrow, her spine coiled inward, her hunting tools within reach, the earth shepherding her and the animals toward their next dance. The dream flows through me, spirals at my sacrum. I hear her voice among the pine needles like a soft lullaby.

You have more to learn from her alive.

❦

"BEDDED IN THE subconscious are recognizable kernels—elements of longer narratives, recurring symbols, cultural remnants. These kernels reference portions of lost, older cultural stories and were identified as snippets that could potentially carry forward such elements basic to myths in transition," muses Shelley

Armitage, a scholar, author, and longtime friend of my west Texas family, exploring how we make meaning through our connection with land, how we cultivate and embody a sense of place.

Recognizable kernels. Older cultural stories. The subconscious. Myths in transition.

The moon and me, earth and sky, we dream each other through the hunt, tracking myths of transition, looking ahead to where the animals are going, behind, to where we've been.

Tracking transformation. Making maps. Mapping myths.

❦

THE ELK'S BREATH at my neck, in my ear. I listen for her approach. Her scent emanates from the earth, swirls in directionless wind, penetrates me. Neither here nor there, she is everywhere.

Let her come, let her show herself. Let her stand there, broadside, open, innocent. I am ready. I listen for what she allows, what she chooses that's beyond the bounds of reason.

Death rests at my fingertips. Life resides in my womb.

But this time the trigger lies locked.

I feed myself, wild. And free.

The forest is quiet. Ponderosa needles blanket the ground. I'm on another elk hunt. So many elk hunts over time, so much ground covered. Just as the sun illuminates the red, vanilla-scented ponderosa trunks, I see a shadow on the ground ahead. It's an elk. She's lying down on the slope across from me at the edge of light.

I watch her. She's relaxed, breathing deeply. I see her warm air make steam through her nostrils. I approach. She watches me, unalarmed.

I walk up, crouch down on my knees, put the rifle down. She rolls onto her side, exposing her chest and soft belly.

I place my right hand over her heart. She allows my touch. I feel her pulse, warm, alive.

I rest there with her, my hand on her heart.

ACKNOWLEDGMENTS

I bow with gratitude to our one great Mother, she who generously gives and inspires beyond all space and time. I owe my life to her and her other-than-human creations. Water. Soil. Animal. Plant. Thank you, divine Earth.

To the dream maker, thank you, for wending your way to and through me, and for saving my life.

Thank you to the Indigenous peoples whose lineage connects and extends through all facets of place, who came long before me and who continue to call these lands home. I am a humble visitor trying to listen and learn.

So many dear friends, family members, and ancestors have helped support, strengthen, and realize these stories. You believed in me each step of the way. Thank you.

Special thanks go to Marsha and Arthur Grantz, my mother and stepfather, for endless love, kindness, and generosity in all forms. To Shaun Green, my brother, with whom I'm enjoying new chapters. To Patty Nagle, whose friendship, boundless support, and raucous laughter have carried me through thick and thin. To Christian Leahy, the midwife wisdom keeper of the stories' souls. She believed and birthed this book into being alongside me, from its conception. Thank you to Leland and Irma Burns, my grandparents who modeled unconditional love, and to Geraldine Lewis Green and my matriarchal lineage of grace and strength. Deep thanks to my aunt and uncle, Marty and Chris Burns, who believe in and love family above all else, and who read on, even still.

Many people read and considered the manuscript over the course of its evolution, helping listen for truth. Thank you Lisa

Pence, Janie Chodosh, Briana Olson, Margie and Stephen Hughes, Susanna Space, Adrienne Harvitz, Julie Wayman, Jude Deason, Ed Myers, Ben Trollinger, Tim Carrier, and Holly Morris.

To my dear friend Tracy Seidman, who showed me how to balance beauty and grit, humor and steadfastness. Her artful hand and wise patience taught me about proportion. You are sorely missed. Thank you.

I extend a warm embrace of profound gratitude to Al Tagestad, for all we have shared. And surrendered. Your generous teaching and loving hold me gently, without constraint. Our discovery continues.

Olivia, the one bright pearl, thank you for coming to me and showing me the world anew. You bring me to life each day.

Lastly, thank you to Sonia Dickey and the University of New Mexico Press for believing in me, these stories, and, most importantly, the necessary voices and supreme intelligence of the animals and their habitats.

Some chapters of this book were previously published in the following publications:

Dark Mountain: "Five Deer" (published as "Blood Bone Oil Water in Dark Mountain")
Edible New Mexico: "Turkey Tail" (published as "Confluence: Life and Death at Water's Edge")
The New Farmer's Almanac: "$1.67"
Waxing and Waning: "New Moon Elk"